Praise for *My M*

"Mentors can make you or break you. My friend, Donna Johnson has chosen the mentor of all mentors. To make your life phenomenally lucrative, fun, and meaningful read this book and make her mentor yours—too."

Mark Victor Hansen,
Co-creator of the *Chicken Soup for the Soul* Series

"Known by many as 'The Mentor' over a career that has spanned nearly three decades, I have never read a single book that covers the topic of Mentorship as effectively as *My Mentor Walks on Water!* Donna covers every angle and wrings out every drip of life-changing value a mentoring relationship can bring into someone's life and business. All while masterfully directing people towards the most important Mentoring relationship any of us can have and it's the only one that comes with the ultimate gift of eternal life!"

Keith Kochner,
Founder/CEO of Mentorship Mastery

"This is such a needed book. It explains concepts that are so needed in today's world, and Donna does an amazing job driving the points home in ways anyone could understand. I like to say, 'Refusing mentorship from Holy Spirit is like cutting your grass with scissors and saying no to a lawn mower.'"

Ray Higdon,
CEO Higdon Group

"Our world needs this book right now! Donna's friendship and leadership through the years has fueled my own career and coaching success. In this book, she does a beautiful job of nourishing the reader with gospel truths, while sharing valuable wisdom in faith, family, and business from her life's journey. Her words are rich encouragement to step out of the boat and lean into the best mentor and friend we could hope for... Jesus."

Toi Stepp,
Actress, Entrepreneur, and Founder of
"Stepping Up With Toi"

"Bravo! Brilliant! *My Mentor Walks on Water* splendidly shows the truth that the Church is the followers of Jesus, the greatest mentor, and not a building. Ministry is your everyday life, not just on Sunday mornings. This book effectively serves as a 'how to' manual to impact and mentor in everyday life. Donna Johnson has done it again—taken what life has handed her and used it to glorify God, bless and lead people. Proud to call her a peer in ministry and friend for forty years."

Bob Lenz,
President and Chief Visionary of Life Promotions

"With *My Mentor Walks on Water*, you see the partnership is different than with any other mentor. And you no longer feel isolated because you're never alone. A must read! This book brings clarity to your life and purpose. We all need a mentor like Donna!"

Stacy Woodford,
Author of *Work from Home Survival Kit for Christian Moms*

"*My Mentor Walks on Water* speaks boldly about a new definition of success and mentorship in today's world. Donna points a clear path to the One mentor who can help you build the life of significance you are meant for."

Janelle Bruland,
Award-winning author of *The Success Lie*

"Through the use of intriguing stories and relevant scriptures, Donna takes on a journey of learning more about who Jesus is, the unconditional love he has for all of us, and how to find our true identity in Him. This is a must-read book for anyone that wants to begin or strengthen their relationship with our Lord and Savior."

Jerry Roisentul,
Owner/CEO, Champion Mentorship, Inc.

"Bold scripture truths with practical help and reflection questions that make us think and ponder our life and those that mentor us! A great tool for our life journey with Jesus!"

Cheryl A Bailey,
Entrepreneur, and author of
12 Life Lessons from the Bible for Kids!

"I am pleased to endorse this amazing book by Donna Johnson. The title itself is of course unforgettable and lays a foundation and sets a compass point that can only lead to a desirable outcome. Donna speaks through her own life experiences which brings the real pop to what the title suggests. The primary mentor must be Jesus. All other mentoring flows from this priority. Jesus as a mentor will always be calling us out of the boat of comfort and limited possibilities. Beyond this foundation, this book is just full of the wisdom of a practitioner and not just the inspiration and idealism of a theoretician. A very key chapter for me is the one on finding your place in one or more of the seven spheres/mountains of society... Donna's own journey and her very practical and powerful equipping tools will ignite and guide you to your own 'walking on water' reality. Get this book and then read this book for its catalytic capabilities for your own life."

Johnny Enlow,
Speaker, Social Reformer and author of
The 7 Mountain Prophecy, Becoming a Superhero,
and *RISE: A Reformer's Guide to the 7 Mountains*

"*My Mentor Walks on Water* isn't 'by' Donna Johnson, it 'is' Donna Johnson. If she had told me the book entirely wrote itself in a single night, I would have believed her. Donna opens herself up to the world throughout this timeless tome, and trusts that her vulnerability will reveal her strengths rather than her weaknesses. And she succeeds with both grace and candor. Although this is a deeply spiritual book, I believe it will appeal to every reader regardless of their beliefs, for the wisdom it imparts transcends religious dogma, and allows the reader to find their own spiritual path, as Donna has… a path, that has beautifully served her and those of us who are fortunate enough to call her 'friend'."

Mark Fournier,
Emmy Award-winning filmmaker

"In *My Mentor Walks on Water*, Donna Johnson shares her personal heartfelt journey with discovering and walking in her faith. It is a true gift and guide for us all. In her words, 'God is not a vending machine. Instead of praying to bless our plans, ask God to reveal to you His plan for your life… My priorities are such that God is first, so how the world wants me to behave is really none of my business.' Seeking and allowing God to be her mentor has allowed Donna to become a fabulous mentor and a shining example of 'living in faith' to thousands."

Sharon Lechter,
Master Business Mentor, author of
Think and Grow Rich for Women and Co-author of
Exit Rich, Outwitting the Devil, Three Feet from Gold
and *NYT bestseller, Rich Dad, Poor Dad*

"In the spiritually uplifting *My Mentor Walks on Water*, Donna Johnson presents the reader with an immediately helpful guide for today's living that is both practical and wonderfully inspirational. With its perfectly-aimed tools, self-quizzes, and scriptural foundation, this book is life-changing from the inside out."

Shad Helmstetter,
Ph.D., Author

"*My Mentor Walks on Water* captures the fingerprints of influence and the ripple effect our walk and witness create. If you are searching for an inspiring way to bring God's design into your day to day, look no further."

Scott Hogle,
President iHeartMedia Honolulu
and bestselling author of *Divine Intelligence*

"I have had many mentors in my life and I have been a mentor to many others. Mentorship is imperative to becoming successful in our life's journey. There is no better mentor than Jesus, the Ultimate Mentor. He created life and knows how it should be lived! *My Mentor Walks on Water* is a tremendous book focusing on Jesus and His ways. Read it, but even more importantly, live it!"

Chris Widener,
Bestselling author of
The Angel Inside and *The Art of Influence*

"Donna took me under her wings as a mentor of mine when I was brand new to my business, even though I joined a different company than hers. I had no mentor and sought her out at an industry event. She even invited my team and me to her home for a lunch meeting when I hosted a retreat in Arizona. Donna is legendary in our industry, not only for her accomplishments, and her legacy and longevity in her company and career—but because of who she is and her heart. She has set the standard of what it is to be a gracious leader, exemplifying how a rising tide lifts us all.

I can wholeheartedly say that I recommend Donna's book on mentorship, as I would not be where I am today without her mentorship. I am where I am today—and who I am today—because of her. I am excited to not only share this book with those I mentor, but also give it as a gift to my team."

Sarah Robbins,
Network Marketing Leader and author of
Rock Your Network Marketing Business

MY MENTOR WALKS ON WATER

SPIRIT-LED MENTORSHIP IN EVERY AREA OF YOUR LIFE

DONNA JOHNSON

MADE FOR SUCCESS

Made for Success Publishing
P.O. Box 1775 Issaquah, WA 98027
www.MadeForSuccess.com

Distributed by Made for Success Publishing

First Printing

Library of Congress Cataloging-in-Publication data

Johnson, Donna
    MY MENTOR WALKS ON WATER: Spirit-Led Mentorship in Every Area of Your Life

        p. cm.

LCCN: 2022920868
ISBN: 978-1-64146-755-1 *(Paperback)*
ISBN: 978-1-64146-756-8 *(eBook)*
ISBN: 978-1-64146-757-5 *(Audiobook)*

Printed in the United States of America

For further information contact Made for Success Publishing
+1(425) 526-6480 or email service@madeforsuccess.net

TABLE OF CONTENTS

ACKNOWLEDGEMENTS

A SPECIAL THANKS to my beautiful Wednesday morning Bible Study Community. We have grown together as we walk in friendship, faith, and obedience. A special thank you to Toi Stepp, Stacy Woodford, Lynda Theis, Jessie Steinkamp, Karen Priemer, and Sue Griz for assisting with Reflection Questions, Scripture sourcing, edits, and prayers.

To my savior Jesus, more than a Mentor.
You walk on water and simply invite us to COME.
To my husband Thomas, your love, faith, and courage
inspire me to step out of the boat with you.

FOREWORD

DONNA JOHNSON HAS been one of my dearest and most remarkable friends for nearly 40 years, and for good reason. As a keynote speaker and author, I have shared stages with some of the most prolific speakers in the world, such as Tony Robbins, Sir Richard Branson, Deepak Chopra, and Donna Johnson, to name a few. I have spoken and trained for some of the biggest corporations in the world, and it has been a very rewarding career. But what I treasure the most is receiving a card or letter from someone telling me that I have helped them in some way. In fact, those letters and cards are so important to me that I have literally filled a bathtub in my home with them. I enjoy reading what people have to say, hearing their stories and how I have helped them in some way, shape, or form.

And that is precisely how I met Donna Johnson. Donna had watched an infomercial where I spoke about my book, "Making Time, Making Money," and we were offering it as an audio series. Donna ordered the tapes and took the time to send a handwritten letter to let me know what a difference I had made in her life. Her letter caught my attention as she described some challenges she had as a single mom and how this series changed her perspective.

"Yesterday is a canceled check, tomorrow is a promissory note, today is the 'present'… that you give to yourself."

If someone hasn't told you yet, this is why you were put on this Earth: to use your God-given talents to change lives. But as I have learned, sometimes the life you change is yours. This is one of the many reasons I love what I do because I have the opportunity to meet seemingly ordinary people like Donna that go on to do extraordinary things. Over several decades of friendship, I have watched Donna overcome obstacles, face difficult circumstances, and achieve great success. Donna has always had a servant heart; no matter how successful she has become, and she has remained humble. That is exactly why she has had success: She put God first, family second, and her business third. Over the years, I have seen how her faith in God has grown and transformed her heart, her business, and the lives of those she has served.

When you have a servant heart, God will direct your steps—or, in my case, cause you to use words you did not plan to say and have never used before in the middle of a speech. I recall saying the phrase, "my mentor walks on water," but I don't really know where it came from. However, God knew this was meant for Donna because He had plans for her to write a book, and she needed the words to inspire her. God is in the miracle business, after all, and He performs them when you put Him first.

It is clear to me that we must never underestimate the impact our words can have on another person. After my nearly four decades of knowing Donna Johnson, I have seen first-hand how my words have impacted her life, how her words have impacted mine, and the impact she is having on thousands of lives.

My Mentor Walks on Water is a book that will change your life... *if* you let it. What I love most is how it walks you through what a real relationship with God looks like, clearing up the confusion about Jesus and what it means to be one of His followers. Who wouldn't want to have help with that? Well, many of you may find yourself confused because you have never understood what it all means and you were too embarrassed to ask. For those of you who may have had a bad experience with religion growing up or consider yourself to be a faithful person but don't know what it's like to fully surrender to God and walk in the freedom of whom He has called you to be, this book is for you.

The reality is that every one of us will face difficulties, tragedies, and crossroads, and sometimes we seek the advice of people that are more messed up than we are. But for those that are really ready to change their circumstances, I can say without a doubt that when you learn how God sees you, "the way you see things" will change. If you have ever wondered if there was more to life than where you are right now, I know with absolute certainty this book will open your eyes to a mentor that walks on water.

I have been sharing this message for over five decades now: The world needs more people who understand their value and worth. *My Mentor Walks on Water* will show you just how valuable you are, how Jesus sees you, how that applies to mentorship, and what it looks like to leave a lasting legacy that ripples throughout the Earth.

Don't miss this invitation because there are men and women waiting on you to make a difference.

—Rita Davenport
Bestselling Author, Speaker, and Entrepreneur

INTRODUCTION

IT STARTED AS a simple memory that scrolled across my newsfeed from several years ago. One of my mentors, Rita Davenport (author of "Laugh Your Way to Success"), my husband, Thomas, and I trained at a leadership event where Tony Robbins was a speaker. While the three of us were in the audience watching Tony, Rita started laughing so hard she had to sit down.

"What's happening?!" I asked her.

Turns out she'd never seen Tony speak in person. "This is what they pay him all this money for? To have everyone hit sticks and jump up and down?" She was in and out of fits of laughter.

When it was Rita's turn to take the stage, in her usual southern, humorous drawl, she said, "What are you all doing jumping up and down, hitting sticks together? Didn't y'all's parents teach you to behave?" The audience roared in laughter.

"And what's all this walking-on-fire nonsense?" Even more laughter (and a few cackles).

Then, in picture-perfect timing, she simply looked up to the heavens, paused, then pointed up and said, "I want you to know that *my* mentor walks on water."

And that's when it happened. In a split second, from a simple social media memory, Holy Spirit downloaded the message I am about to share with you in the following pages. Until that moment, writing a book was the furthest thought from my mind. While I've contributed to articles, written collaborations, and been featured in many books and publications, I never thought that I would be the one writing the book you are now reading.

After stumbling upon the social media memory, I immediately called Rita to ask her where the "my mentor walks on water" statement came from. To my knowledge, she had never used that phrase before, and I had been friends with her for decades! She told me that she had no idea where it came from and that she never said it again. She then encouraged me to follow God's prompting for this message to be written.

God made it very clear to me that this was not going to be a watered-down, lukewarm approach to mentorship, but rather a radical encounter with Biblical truth that has stood the test of time, yet very few participate in.

For some time, I've been noticing a surge in people seeking direction and guidance in this crazy world. With the onset of the Internet and a growing disillusionment with institutional religion, most people dismiss Jesus as simply a good person, a teacher, or even a fable. So many people walk around confused, questioning the validity of the idea that Jesus is anything more than a character created by religion. Our culture glorifies selfies, personal image, and celebrity status, while social media, television shows, and movies are hyper-focused on murder, the occult, demons, and putting religion in a bad light. As a result, people turn to the self-help industry to find guidance. There's a concerted effort to diminish or erase Jesus in every aspect of one's culture—to the point that even people who have grown up in a family that went to church every Sunday have become confused and disillusioned.

My intention for this book is to clear the fog of confusion, to give you a clear picture of the truth. Yes, *the* truth. Not my opinion, but the proven word of God that cannot be disputed. Many have tried; all have failed.

SO, WHY MENTORSHIP?

"Donna, what are you writing about?" my friends and family asked after I told them I was writing a book. I responded with "Faith-based mentorship," but it didn't feel right. I knew I was going to need a clearer, more concise description.

While taking a shower, I asked God to give me a better picture of what this description might be. The reply came immediately: "God-ordained, Spirit-led mentorship in every area of your life."

"What?!" I responded, flabbergasted and unsure if I heard correctly. And again, I heard Him say, "God-ordained, Spirit-led mentorship in every area of your life!"

I nearly slipped out of the shower as I rushed to write the phrase down. It just didn't make any sense to me. *I mean, I'm not a pastor, so how is this ordained?* I thought.

While still dripping wet, I searched Google to find the meaning of *God-ordained.* Here's what popped up:

"God orders, appoints or commands one to do something that is set apart and special."

I knew then that God had divinely appointed this book for you to read, share, and start a Spirit-led mentorship movement. We are all called to action: to be "Water Walkers."

So, where does mentorship begin? Do we purposefully seek out mentors, or do we just let life happen? What you value and how you want to live your life should be well thought out, not just happen haphazardly. I believe mentorship—and any relationship with a coach or advisor you align with for influence—starts with having a clear understanding of *who* you are, *why* it matters, *what* your identity is built on, and *how* you would like to experience a life of abundance.

When you observe a lofty skyscraper under construction, you don't see any progress for a very long time. That's because, much of the time, construction is focused on establishing the bedrock and foundation of the structure. So it is with your life. If you think of yourself as a skyscraper under construction, you'll need to contemplate and plan your blueprint for a firm foundation—your "who" and your "why."

In Section One, we will explore questions about *who* you are and *who* your fellow Water Walker Jesus is. This is important because it shapes the foundation for your worldview and the choices you make for not only being influenced, but influencing others.

This is the *why*. Always know your why.

After we've established the *who* and *why*, in Section Two, we explore the *how* in how we are mentored. Looking forward to Section Three, we'll discuss the results (fruit)—the *what*—and how it affects every area of your life. How you do anything is how you do everything. And lastly, in Section Four, you'll learn what it means to be a Water Walker and how to become a person of influence, creating a ripple effect.

Learning to grow and mature in wisdom will feel much like you're moving from being an amateur to a pro, from mastery to legacy living. Think of it like a sandwich. The bottom bread is the *foundation* of your beliefs and worldview. The middle or meat of the sandwich is the *source* of how you are mentored and influenced, and the top bread is the *evidence*, the *application,* and *mastery* in all areas of your life.

My husband Thomas likes to start a book by flipping through to chapters that catch his eye, and sometimes will even read a book backward. He was reading these chapters as I was writing them, and about halfway through, he told me how much he loved the way everything was tying and flowing together. "This is definitely not a book that I can read backward," he said, and I recommend the same for you.

Start from the beginning and watch how God moves. I pray that this book inspires you to seek out wise mentorship along your journey. Today is the first day of the rest of your life. Give yourself grace to start *this day* and move forward in the direction God has ordained for you.

I challenge you to read this book from two perspectives: *Grow Me; Serve You,* which leads to *Reflection; Ripple Effect.*

1. GROW ME (Reflection): Reflect on how you can grow
2. SERVE YOU (Ripple Effect): Envision how you can serve others.

In each chapter, you'll have the opportunity to both grow personally and apply that growth to serve the people around you. As you're learning about mentorship, you can actively mentor others—you don't have to wait until you've "got it all together." (What does that even mean, anyway?) You can apply the principles in this book right away and grow to serve others—where you're tempted to stay in the boat, where it's comfortable, you have a choice to step out. That's where the growth really happens and the ripples reach far and wide.

So, what do you say? Are you ready to step out of the boat and walk on water?

THE FOUNDATION OF MENTORSHIP

Chapter 1

WHO DO YOU THINK YOU ARE?

NO MATTER WHAT your age or circumstances, it's never too late to be at peace with knowing who you truly are—not what the world tells us we should be, or whom people expect us to be. After all, we will meet hundreds, if not thousands, of people in our lifetime, but the one person we are with every single moment is *ourselves*!

"Everywhere I go, there I am!"

But why is that important? And why are we talking about it at the beginning of a book about mentorship? Well, what you believe about yourself is like the key that starts the engine of your car. And how you see yourself will determine the route you take on your journey of life.

What roadmap will *you* follow?

A positive, loving view of yourself (self-identity) then creates positive choices for a healthy well-being. For example, just a simple agreement you make to be good to yourself in every way means that you will take care to watch your thought processes and make good choices for self-care, nutrition, and exercise. On the flip side, a negative view of yourself often results in feelings of unworthiness. Because you feel unworthy, you will expect to fail, which often leads to living a neutral life, and not setting goals or plans to improve it. I call this cycle "living in your comfort zone." Or worse, you may subconsciously self-sabotage.

A strong sense of identity will not only build confidence and clarity, but will also help to keep you from morphing into whom someone else says you are or wants you to be. Knowing who you are will also shape your choices and priorities. You'll discover what matters most to you; what brings you joy and purpose. You'll start seeing a pattern of cause and effect. Things that are positive and loving will yield a pleasant sense of well-being, while destructive choices create negative consequences. This is a lifelong process, so don't wait for your deathbed to reconcile this important question: "Who do you think you are?"

I often say, "I'm not the person I *used* to be, and I'm not the person I'm *going* to be." I feel like I am always "under construction," but life is all about progress over perfection.

TRAUMA DOESN'T HAVE TO DEFINE YOU

Knowing who you are matters. In fact, I was on a roller coaster ride much of my life because I failed to take the time to really understand who I was—who God says that I am. As I journeyed through the process of self-discovery, I identified two key influences that kept me from truly understanding who I am and being at peace with how God sees me.

The first was believing something was wrong with me if I wasn't perfect. This belief is incredibly commonplace because, at our core, I believe we want to strive to do the right thing, in the right way, for the right reason. In reality, however, we are in a fallen world with free will, and we will never be perfect, even when we try our hardest. Setting that expectation for myself was setting myself up for failure, which made me feel that I was not worthy of happiness or success.

When I finally began to understand that I am human and have fallen short and that God's grace was sufficient for me, I learned to be at peace with all of me—even the imperfections. And, of course, when you love yourself, you can love others as Christ loves us.

The other major influence that affected how I saw myself was listening too intently to what other people said about me. Our upbringing has a significant influence on who we think we are, whether it be our circumstances or the people in our lives. We may identify ourselves as our work, our title, or our accomplishments—or lack thereof. This influences not only how we feel about ourselves, but how we interact with others. Often, when we have a warped view of who we are and attempt to identify with our accomplishments or status, we will seek validation and approval from others, which is an exhausting set-up for disaster.

In my case, it was my earthly father.

His words cut like a knife. And it wasn't just the words; it was the smirky smile, beady eyes and an evil attitude of *I know who you are*—something a little girl should never experience. My dad used to horse around and play with my four brothers, but for my mom and me, it was different.

My earliest memory of my father not being like other dads was when I was 5 years old. I was playing with a friend, and her mom painted our fingernails pink. I was elated, and when I went home to show my family, my dad called me a whore. I later had to ask my mom what that word even meant.

But it didn't stop there.

As the only girl in the family, I had my own room, while my brothers shared a bedroom. One night, a storm was rolling in, and my younger brother Greg was afraid of the thunder and lightning. He came to my room in tears, and I consoled him. When my dad heard about it the next morning, he was furious and accused me of being inappropriate with my brother.

I didn't know it at the time, but my father suffered from severe abuse as a child, which caused him to be a misogynist— he had a strong hatred for women. He was later diagnosed with paranoid schizophrenia when he divorced my mother and left our family. I was 13 years old when he left for California to pursue riches, never once sending child support to my mother; meanwhile, he told my brothers that the state would take care of us. As kids, my brothers and I worked to help our mom put food on the table, and I remember my grandpa paying the local dairy to deliver milk and eggs every week because we didn't have enough money for groceries.

The negative messaging I received during my childhood made me even more determined to prove my father wrong, and

I excelled in everything I did. Beginning in high school—and through early adulthood—I competed nationally in swimming and coached at the YMCA, high school, and university levels. I could also type as fast as I talk, which serves me to this day! Funny enough, a few years after graduation, I was the swimming coach at the high school I attended. One day, my old typing teacher saw me in the hallway.

"Double D!" (That was my nickname comprised of the letters of my first and last name.) "You still hold the typing record!"

During high school, I was the president of the Pep Club, where I led school spirit pep rallies. Oh, and I was also the president of Davitas Synchronized Swim Club! My desire to achieve has always been there. Being raised in a family that didn't encourage or couldn't afford a college education, I used my talents of swimming, typing, and leadership to pursue three careers at the same time: swim coach, secretary, and a consultant for a direct sales company.

Still, I struggled with the words my father had spoken into my heart. They haunted me, and I felt as though they continued to chase after me throughout my life. Even though none of it made sense, and the labels weren't true, I found myself believing they were. When trauma happens at a young age, it affects your critical thinking skills. But I didn't stay there forever. I did the work, and it paid off.

As we journey through life, especially after trauma, we can remain stuck in an unhealthy identity, choosing to believe the labels of who other people say we are, or we can choose to do the work. Don't buy into the lie that it can't be done. It's not only possible, it's worth it. There is hope for a better life, and I'm a testament to that fact.

BE A VICTOR, NOT A VICTIM

After going through a divorce with three small children, I
needed help. I found a Christian counseling program and spent
a week-long retreat working on my personal healing. During
the counseling sessions, my therapist learned that my dad was
in town for a class reunion and invited him to do a session with
me. Fear gripped me as I anticipated sitting in the same room
with him. He hadn't spoken to me for years and had never
even bothered to meet my three children—his grandchildren.

On the day of the appointment, as he sat across from me,
terror swept through my body as I felt like that little girl with
my accuser. He thanked my counselor for inviting him and
then went on to rant about what a horrible human being I
was. To my shock, my counselor just smiled and nodded her
head as he spoke. She never said a word. Finally, after about
15 minutes, she stood up, reached out to shake his hand, and
said, "Thank you so much for joining us today," and escorted
him out the door.

My mind was racing. *What in the world just happened?* I
was literally shaking in disbelief.

She nearly had to pick me up off the floor. However, what
happened next would eventually be the catalyst for my healing.
She said, "I could not engage with your dad because it was
obvious to me that he has severe psychological issues. He is
not well, and I was *not* going to allow him to abuse you. I just
needed him to leave. "

It was the first time someone had intervened for me. She
explained that the trauma I experienced as a little girl was not
my fault and demonstrated setting a boundary that I would

eventually learn to put into place and practice myself. I began to understand not only *why* this was important, but *how* to do it. I learned to stop listening to what my earthly father told me about who I was and listened to the voice of truth—who God says I am. It felt like a new dance move that I had to learn, and all the movements felt awkward at first until they became a habit. However, eventually, my journey brought me to a healthy understanding of who I am, based on the loving, heavenly Father: God. In this, I have peace in knowing who I am.

FORGIVENESS, BOUNDARIES, AND STORIES

To *forgive* is a key factor in your healing journey toward understanding who you really are. As has been said by many different people, unforgiveness is like drinking poison and expecting the other person to die. However, other people's actions fall wholly on themselves, and we do not have to accept them. Let me be clear from the get-go: to forgive someone does NOT mean that what they did is OK, and is different than reconciliation. You can forgive someone yet still maintain healthy boundaries in not talking to or subjecting yourself to them. But we must remember that healing isn't about forgetting what's happened to us; it's about not letting it define us. To *forget* disregards the lesson.

As I practiced new ways to see myself by setting boundaries and growing my self-esteem, I felt a sense of sadness and compassion toward my father. I eventually learned about some of the traumas my father experienced in his own upbringing, and I mourned not having a healthy relationship with my father, but, at the same time, I was grateful to end a generational cycle of abuse.

Whether your forgiveness journey involves some level of physical or emotional abuse caused by someone else or not, everyone has a story. Maybe you did something that you haven't been able to forgive yourself for. Or perhaps you have done the work and forgiven yourself, but others still hold it against you. Whatever it looks like, I encourage you to seek healing.

When we talk about relational conflict, whether it's with other people or within ourselves, it's important to note that there's a difference between shame and conviction. Shame—feelings like unworthiness, self-hatred, or accusatory thoughts—is from the enemy to keep you down. Conviction, on the other hand, is a healthy reaction given by the Holy Spirit to affect us toward change and repentance. The voice of conviction is *not* condemning. Conviction is loving, as it turns you back toward the Lord, who is love!

Take some time to discover your own story. If someone were to write a book about your life, what would be told about you? It's OK to process and reflect on your life to discover the lessons through the good times *and* the tough stuff. It all shapes us into who we choose to be. What internal work do you need to do to process your upbringing or circumstances for a healthy view of yourself?

REWORD AND REWIRE

Negative self-talk and habits are like ruts in an old-fashioned record: the needle is stuck in the groove. My friend Keith Kochner, founder of Mentorship Mastery, teaches a two-day workshop called The Exchange. Fifteen years ago, I had the opportunity to attend this uniquely life-changing event. During the workshop, we focused on the process of detoxing unhealthy stories and replacing them with loving, healing stories to create new habits and self-talk. For instance, I was writing a story in my mind that I was not worthy of success and happiness. My dad was looming over me in my subconscious mind, shaming me. Just like detoxing our body from unhealthy toxins, I needed to "detox" my stinking thinking.

In order to grow, you've got to stop accepting, tolerating, and settling for what you don't want and start learning how to create what you *do* want in your life and business. Working on a healthy self-image will help you stop the self-sabotage. It is foolish to keep doing the same things and expecting different results. You cannot walk toward your greatness; you can only walk away from it because we are all made in God's image.

There are many practical resources for this type of internal work, but I would highly recommend looking into Keith's exchange event. I have also found a lot of incredible information and practical tools in my friend Dr. Shad Helmstetter's classic book, "What to Say When You Talk to Yourself." He says:

"You will become what you think about most; your success or failure in anything, large or small, will depend on your programming—what you accept from others, and what you say when you talk to yourself."

We teach people how to treat us, and it starts with our own self-talk. It was only when I began believing a new script and re-writing my stories that my self-talk started to change, and I found it easier to respond to everyday circumstances in a healthy way. It's important to surround yourself with people who not only respond in a positive manner to your journey of healthy self-image but are working on their own self-development as well. Over the years, those around me—not just my children and family, but also business associates—have corrected statements I've made and kept me aligned with the stories I wanted to tell myself. For instance, a reaction that might typically be, "Oh, I can't do that; I am *so* afraid of heights," would be challenged with, "Be careful with what you say!" or "How can you reword that?" To which I would respond, "I used to be afraid of heights, but now I am getting braver each time I feel that fear."

The following is a common conversation that my husband and I have while he's driving and I'm in the passenger seat. (If you're in a relationship or married, you probably know where I'm going with this already!)

I often tell him about how frightened my mother was of heights and driving; that she was not even able to drive on highways because she was so frightened to merge. As kids, if we got anywhere near the edge of a cliff, like at the Grand Canyon, she would literally hyperventilate. This has been a generational fear that I've had to work on, and it's even been passed down to my children. My oldest son, Nathaniel, was with me in Arizona and we were visiting schools, as he was between college and grad school. We went for breakfast between tours, where he announced he wanted to take a hot air balloon ride. My immediate response was, "Oh, I would *never* do that!"

He was quick to answer, "Mom, you literally teach people how to overcome their fears by using self-talk. Let's do it!"

How could I say no to *that*?

Was that an easy hot air balloon ride? I'll bet you know the answer to that question. After practically laying on the base of the basket at the start, I slowly stood up and decided to enjoy this peaceful, beautiful experience. Our pilot instructed that a small percentage of landings don't go well. To our surprise, our landing was one of those rough landings, skipping across the desert and into cacti. We had a choice about how to respond, so we just laughed and had a fun story to share. I've since gone on several hot air balloon rides to help overcome my fears.

Habits and self-talk can stay with you for a lifetime, so it's important to start doing something about it now. How can you reframe or exchange the words that come out of your mouth? I encourage you to practice listening to your internal self-talk, but be careful with what you say about those around you as well.

Recently, I met a young mom with her two-year-old son clinging to her leg. I knelt down to his eye level to smile and speak with him. The mother quickly jumped in to say, "Oh, he's really shy. He won't talk to you."

I nodded yet continued to speak with him gently until a smile and an interaction emerged from him. The mom was genuinely touched by my effort to connect with her son on his level. We had a really lovely exchange, and she realized that those little ears were listening to the prophecy she spoke of him.

Another great example is one I've called, "Alex hates to cook." I have five adult children, and, like my husband and me, they all love to cook. In our home, the kitchen is our happy place. My youngest are my twin daughters Liv and Alex. Growing up, Liv loved to cook, but Alex didn't. We would tease Alex and say, "Liv cooks and Alex cleans up." Alex would joke back, "Nope. Liv cooks and Alex eats." This was all in good fun, but what I didn't realize is how our conversations kept her in this belief about herself.

Years later, in her early 20s, Alex called to have a serious conversation with me. "Mom, remember how you all used to talk about cooking, and you used to say that I don't like to cook? Well, can we change that conversation? Because I've decided that I am starting to really love cooking."

Wow! Busted in my own teaching.

As you can see, it's never too late to flip the script and change the way we speak over each other and ourselves. This is also a great time to remind you to be good to yourself. Having a sense of humor and learning to laugh always lightens the lesson.

PROGRESS, NOT PERFECTION

God loves you and has a purpose for your life, but the enemy wants to keep this truth away from you. I encourage you to take some time to make your own exchange, like the ones I wrote about in the previous sections. First, write down the stories and self-talk that don't serve you. This could be anything from "I don't like to cook" to "I have to be perfect" to "I'll never be good enough." Then burn them, throw them away, or flush them down the toilet. Now, you must leave those stories and thoughts behind. When the old tapes want to play, cancel that thought! Commit yourself to learning new patterns of speaking about yourself and others. In time, your new self-talk will become a habit, and your old ways will seem foreign to you when they pop up. Give yourself grace to process a new language of living, loving, and learning.

Sometimes, when going through the work of learning new patterns, it's helpful to close your eyes and picture a beautiful setting. Right now, I am writing at our home on one of the islands of Sweden, surrounded by the soothing sea and lush forest with the harmonious sound of birds and wildlife. There's a pillow on the bench next to me that reads, "This Is My Happy Place." Hopefully, from here on out, your transformation will feel like you're being transported to your happy place. Imagine that the pain you've experienced in your life was a rest stop of lessons on your journey; a place to *visit* but not a place to *live*.

A few years ago, I offered an incentive in my direct marketing business to bring two couples on a sailing trip in the British Virgin Islands. One of the couples who came on the trip, Sue and Larry, expressed that it was the most beautiful vacation they had ever experienced. Two years later, Larry was dying of cancer and asked if it was possible to head back out on our sailboat one last time. He even teased that, "If I die while sailing, just throw me overboard because I'll be in my happy place." Miraculously, when he stepped on the boat for that trip, his health was the best it had been since his diagnosis. To see him at such peace with God and nature was a gift. I asked him how he was handling everything, and his response was beautiful. He told me that when he starts to get anxious, he goes into a quiet state of prayer and meditation. With his eyes closed, he exhales for several seconds and holds his breath before inhaling. The most important part is exhaling all the fear, pain, and negative thoughts. Then he inhales God's goodness, peace, and joy. He repeats this for several breaths. What a practice!

Larry died a few weeks later. I now practice this often and share it with others. Having those memories to celebrate his life while alive will be with me forever.

Live like you are dying because *you are*! When and how, God only knows. There's no U-Haul at the end of a hearse, so don't wait for your deathbed to resolve the question we've been looking at throughout the chapter: "Who am I?"

EXERCISE

To get you started on your journey of replacing your old self-talk, here's a chart of a few common lies and a scripture that speaks the truth to flip the script. This will help you pay attention to what you say in comparison to what God says and get you excited for the work we'll do in the next chapter!

YOU SAY	GOD SAYS	BIBLE VERSE
I can't figure it out	I will direct your steps	Proverbs 3:5-6
I'm too tired	I will give you rest	Matthew 11:28-30
It's impossible	All things are possible	Luke 18:27
Nobody loves me	I love you	John 3:16
I can't forgive myself	I forgive you	Romans 8:1
It's not worth it	It will be worth it	Romans 8:28
I'm not smart enough	I will give you wisdom	1 Corinthians 1:30
I'm not able	I am able	2 Corinthians 9:8
I can't go on	My grace is sufficient	2 Corinthians 12:9
I can't do it	You can do all things	Phillippians 4:13
I can't manage	I will supply all your needs	Phillippians 4:19
I'm afraid	I have not given you fear	2 Timothy 1:7
I feel all alone	I will never leave you	Hebrews 13:5

Now it's time to write a new story, one based on who God says you are!

At the end of every chapter, we will have two sets of questions to work through what was presented. They're broken up into two parts: Reflections, which are inward focused, and Ripple Effect, which are outward focused. I encourage you to set aside intentional time to do this work and really ask the Lord to speak to you through the questions.

Water Walker Reflections:

*What incident or incidents happened in your life that you have allowed to grow into a pattern? _____

_____

_____

*Are you allowing something to define you that you need to forgive and let go of? What is it? _____

_____

_____

*What is a VICTIM issue in your life you need to turn into a VICTOR mentality? _____

_____

_____

*Make your own exchange: Where can you rewrite stories that are not serving who God has called you to be? _____

_____

_____

*Review the list above (YOU SAY, GOD SAYS) and highlight the top three "you say" statements that you struggle with, then reflect on the Scripture (what God says).

Top 3:

    1) _____

    2) _____

    3) _____

Ripple Effect:

*How will writing a new story about yourself improve your life? _____

_____

_____

_____

*By doing this work, what impact will it have on your loved ones and those you interact with? _____

_____

_____

_____

Chapter 2

WHO DOES GOD SAY YOU ARE?

> *"I am chosen, not forsaken*
> *I am who You say I am*
> *You are for me, not against me*
> *I am who You say I am."*
>
> —*Hillsong*

AS WE NEAR the end of our life, I would be willing to bet that the majority of us will wrestle with this thought: *I wish I wouldn't have worried so much about what other people think.* Yes, we all inherently want to be respected, valued, loved, and admired, but when we don't have a secure self-identity aligned with God, we will unhealthily seek approval from others.

I want you to picture a rubber ducky bouncing around in a storm, tossed about by the waves in the ocean. That's what your life will be like when your main priority is approval from others. You'll count hearts and likes on social media, seeking validation from external sources. When you find that approval, you feel like you're on top of the world. However, when you don't get the likes or the shout-outs or the follows, you'll feel unsteady, seeking another dopamine hit through social media or shallow friendships to help you feel anchored, when, in reality, you're just getting tossed around.

Now, I want you to picture that same stormy ocean, but this time there is a boat with a strong anchor tethered to it. This is what your life will be like when you know who you are and are tethered to the word of God. You will have an anchor when everything around you feels unsteady and uncertain—you will be able to stand strong in the storm. When you don't get the approval or validation from others, you won't be tossed around like a rubber ducky! You will be able to come back to the anchor and remember what is really true about who you are.

The reality is, God's approval is the only one that matters—the only voice we need to hear. People will come and go, but the *one* who will be with you forever is our Heavenly Father. Knowing this truth can help anchor you in times of trouble, straighten out your priorities, and keep you in the lane He destined you to walk in.

THIS IS WHAT GOD SAYS

Now that we've explored the importance of knowing what God thinks about us and how it anchors us, let's take some time to discover those truths together.

God says we are His beloved Child.

"Beloved" means to be greatly loved, and no one loves us like God—*no one*. Think of the one person you think loves you the most. Maybe it's your husband or wife, or your mother or father. Maybe it's a best friend. As much as that person loves you, God loves you *more*. And unlike earthly relationships, where people can withhold their love from us even though it's not the way it should be, there's nothing we can do that can separate us from His love.

Romans 8:38-39 says, "For I am convinced that neither death, nor life, nor angels, nor principalities, nor things present, nor things to come, nor powers, nor height, nor depth, nor any other created thing will be able to separate us from the love of God that is in Christ Jesus our Lord."

In fact, God sent His very Son, Jesus, to earth because He loved the world so much—because He loved YOU so much! Jesus is the greatest expression of God's love for us, and He died and rose again so that His great love can live *within* us.

"For God so loved the world, that He gave His only Son, so that everyone who believes in Him will not perish, but have eternal life. (John 3:16)

And wait, there's more! This great love has made the way for you to be free! Take a look at this stunning passage from Ephesians, chock full of truth. What other love would give up their very lives for us?

"But God, being rich in mercy, because of His great love with which He loved us, even when we were dead in our wrong-doings, made us alive together with Christ (by grace you have been saved.)" (Ephesians 2:4-5)

This love is so profound that we often don't allow this truth to really sink in. When was the last time you thought about the love of God? When I start praying, my mind sometimes starts racing and I can't concentrate. I've come to learn to take some deep breaths and picture myself entering a peaceful white room with beautiful soft music. When I walk in, I see my Heavenly Father sitting on a white couch. I will often go sit with Him to talk, pray, and ask for His love to fill me to overflowing.

In fact, I'd love for you to do the same. If you're able, close your eyes and imagine that same room. Try to see your Heavenly Father sitting on the couch, and sit down to talk with Him. Ask Him to show you how much He loves you, to pour that love out and melt away any feelings of unworthiness or shame.

God says we are chosen.

Even before He made the world, God loved us and chose us as His own.

"Just as He chose us in Him before the foundation of the world, that we would be holy and blameless before Him. In love He predestined us to adoption as sons and daughters through Jesus Christ to Himself, according to the good pleasure of His will, to the praise of the glory of His grace, with which He favored us in the Beloved." (Ephesians 1:4-6)

Maybe you were born into a family where you were unwanted, abandoned, or mistreated. This is not God's design! I pray that you are comforted by the truth that you are chosen by the creator of the Universe. You are special; you are unique. Unlike the world that embraces a false view to judge and separate us by the color of our skin or our social status, God has created us as individual, multi-faceted children who are part of *His* family. He sees us as one. Pastor Ken Ham, the CEO and founder of Answers in Genesis U.S., the Creation Museum, and the Ark Encounter teaches that the world has lost the Biblical view that teaches we are one race—the human race.

We are all descendants of one man: Adam (the first man God created in the garden of Eden). People love to trace their ancestry, and a recent study by Emory University confirms that children who know their family history are more resilient and confident. While physical ancestry links us to Adam, our spiritual ancestry begins with the saving grace of Jesus. God not only chose us before creation, but He chose Jesus to save us from the fall of Adam and Eve.

God says we are His workmanship.

As we briefly touched on in the last section, we are all uniquely designed; even our own fingerprint shows the care for each individual! We can see this in the creation story in the first few chapters of Genesis: God made us in His image and likeness, and He created male and female differently and uniquely.

However, we often compare ourselves to others—remember the rubber ducky? When we look to (and at) the people around us, we take our eyes off God's design, which was to form us each as a masterpiece!

Ephesians 2:10 says, "For we are His workmanship, created in Christ Jesus for good works, which God prepared beforehand so that we would walk in them."

Look at the inspiring life of Nick Vujicic. Nick has a rare syndrome called tetra-amelia, which means that he was born without arms and legs. From the first time I heard his name, I had been fascinated by his story, so when I heard he was speaking at our church in Arizona, I knew I had to go, and even arrived early to sit near the front. As he shared with vulnerability and authority, we were all in tears as we listened to him speak about choosing to be a victor over a victim. Not only is he happily married with a family, but he also speaks in front of millions of people around the world, sharing his message of hope and inspiration. He challenges people to discover their value and purpose and use it, embracing what makes them feel "different" as something God-ordained.

Are you looking around at everyone else and comparing yourself? You might as well give it up because there's no one like you. I challenge you to take some time to discover the beautiful workmanship God made in you and develop your gift to share with the world.

God says we are His temple.

What comes to mind when you hear the word "temple"? In my mind, I picture a majestic, sacred, ornamental building or church designed for worship and prayer. While there *are* buildings called temples you can attend for this purpose, did you know God says that WE are His temple?

On what we now call Good Friday, Jesus died on the cross for our sins. On Easter Sunday, He rose from the dead and walked among the people, teaching them about the kingdom of God for 40 days before ascending into Heaven. Before He ascended, He said He would send a helper, the Holy Spirit. Ten days later (fifty days after Easter), the Holy Spirit fell upon the believers gathered in the upper room, also known as Pentecost. But what does that have to do with us being a temple? Well, because Jesus ascended and sent us the Holy Spirit, He now dwells in us as followers of Christ. If you've accepted Christ, your body is now a temple for the Holy Spirit!

"Do you not know that you are a temple of God and that the Spirit of God dwells in you?" (1 Corinthians 3:16)

How does it make you feel to know that your body is a temple? I hope it provokes you to be good to yourself and make wise choices for what you allow in your body. Physically, you have choices of what you put in your body and on your skin. Does it fuel or harm you? This includes your other senses, too, like what you listen to, read, and watch. What you allow into your mind and body can fuel you or poison you. You have a choice to treat your body as the temple God made. Notice He didn't use the word "home" or "house"; it's "temple." That means your body is a shrine, so to speak, to be used as a sacred residence for Holy Spirit.

Through the death and resurrection of Jesus, we receive a new identity and new life. He says that we are the righteousness of God in Jesus Christ and a living temple for His Holy Spirit.

1 Corinthians 6:19-20 says, "Or do you not know that your body is a temple of the Holy Spirit within you, whom you have from God, and that you are not your own? For you have been bought for a price: therefore glorify God in your body."

God says we are redeemed; a new person in Christ.

Because of the original sin of our ancestors, Adam and Eve, we need to enter into a covenant with God, for He is holy. A covenant is a promise or agreement between God and man. The Old Testament (also known as the Old Covenant) lays the foundation of what was to come, foreshadowing the coming of a Savior. From Genesis to Malachi, every chapter of the Old Testament lays out our desperate need for a Savior and tells of a people longing for the Messiah. The New Testament (also known as the New Covenant) describes the fulfillment of the Old Covenant through Jesus Christ. He is so rich in kindness and grace that He purchased our freedom, not with gold or silver, but with the very blood of His son Jesus Christ whom he sacrificed for us. When we accept this reality—that Jesus died for our sins—we ask Jesus to forgive us, and we repent (turn away from sin), then we are made new! We are transferred from the kingdom of darkness to the kingdom of light. This explains the term "born again"—we are born once of the flesh, and again by the Spirit.

"Therefore if anyone is in Christ, *this person is* a new creation; the old things passed away; behold, new things have come." (2 Corinthians 5:17)

A common misunderstanding of accepting Jesus and being made new is the belief that now you are perfect from here on out. That is simply not true! You're not expected to be perfect, and you cannot be! There is only one perfect person, and that is Jesus Christ. With the acceptance of Jesus Christ and the Holy Spirit dwelling inside, you will become a new person in Christ.

Ephesians 1:13 says, "In Him, you also, after listening to the message of truth, the gospel of your salvation—having also believed, you were sealed in Him with the Holy Spirit of the promise."

The Ephesians passage above says that the Holy Spirit is a guarantee of our inheritance because our redemption is not yet complete. Galatians 5:5 says that we are waiting by faith for a future righteousness which we do not yet have. God's redemption plan is not finished as we await the second coming of Jesus that is promised. While we are waiting, we are growing and maturing to live a holy life that glorifies God.

God says we are His friend.

When you think about your inner circle of people, make sure God is number one.

Through our relationship with Jesus, God shares His heart with us. We can walk with Him and talk with Him. Moses did this in Exodus 33:11, which says, "So the Lord used to speak to Moses face to face, just as a man speaks to his friend. When Moses returned to the camp, his servant Joshua, the son of Nun, a young man, would not depart from the tent."

How cool is that? Moses asked God not only if he could walk and talk with Him, but to meet with Him face-to-face! Maybe we think today this is impossible. But think about this: in Old Testament times, when you wanted to approach God, you needed an animal sacrifice! And even then, you couldn't see Him face-to-face. Today, we have a new covenant through Jesus and can boldly approach the throne with our praise, prayers, and petitions.

"Therefore, brothers and sisters, since we have confidence to enter the holy place by the blood of Jesus, by a new and living way which He inaugurated for us through the veil, that is, through His flesh, and since we have a great priest over the house of God." (Hebrews 10:19-21)

Some days, you'll be in great need and approach Him on your knees. Other times, you'll simply say, "God, show me Your Glory." I like to pray, "God, reveal to me what is hurting Your heart. Give me Your eyes to see what You see; give me Your ears to hear what You hear."

God isn't a vending machine. As my faith matures, I am spending more time praising and thanking Him and less time asking and petitioning. Just like a friend, be consistent. Don't just come to Him when you are hurting and in need. Make it a habit to not only have your dedicated prayer and devotion time, but also to talk to Him during your day. Can you talk to Jesus like you do your friend over coffee? This is the relationship He wants us to have with Him. Christianity is a relationship, not a religion.

Our world is full of deception and disinformation. Often, friends will come to me and ask, "What do you think of _____?" Maybe it's about a news article they read, wondering if it's true. My standard answer is, "Hmmm. I'm not sure, but I do know someone who *does* know; let's ask Him!" Then we take it to the Lord in prayer.

We're also living in a time when so many are grieving through loss. Whether it's loved ones, sickness, death, possessions, or jobs; people are hurting. I see a couple different reactions. Some people lean into God, seeking guidance and help. Others blame God and turn away feeling either angry, sad, or abandoned. The famous poem "Footprints in the Sand" tells the story of someone who only saw one set of footprints during their trial. When crying out to God, He said, "My Child, that is when I carried you."

"No longer do I call you slaves, for the slave does not know what his master is doing; but I have called you friends, because all things that I have heard from My Father I have made known to you." (John 15:15)

God says we are a member of the body of Christ and His inheritance.

We are designed for fellowship and community. I believe one of the tools in the enemy's toolbox is to socially distance and cover our faces to keep us from God's intention for our lives. We thrive on connection.

During the COVID lockdown in Italy, the University of Foggia performed a study with results showing that more people were affected negatively by the isolation than they were by the disease, even though Italy was hardest hit during this time. We were not designed to live life alone. We were designed to connect and rely on and help each other.

Romans 12:4-5 illustrates this beautifully: "For just as we have many parts in one body and all the body's parts do not have the same function, so we, who are many, are one body in Christ, and individually parts of one another."

We all have different talents, and we shine our brightest when we work hand in hand to help each other while using our unique gifts. When we band together this way, we glorify God and lift each other up. Fellowship is a mutual bond that

Christians have with Christ that puts us in a deep, eternal relationship with one another as equal heirs to His inheritance.

"Therefore you are no longer a slave, but a son; and if a son, then an heir through God." (Galatians 4:7)

* * *

The Bible is perfectly clear about who God says we are. The gospel of Christ is this:

- That we, who are sinful, need a Savior
- That God is infinitely holy and just
- That we are, therefore, under his wrath and condemnation
- But also, that God, in his great mercy, has sent his son Jesus Christ, whose perfect obedience and death in our place makes it possible for God to justify and declare righteous all who trust in Christ
- So that there is, therefore, no condemnation for those who are in Christ Jesus

The more we read Scripture, and the more we walk, talk, and pray with Him, the more we discover how deep and how wide His love is for us. We are transformed into the person God says we are when we make Jesus Christ the pursuit of our lives.

WHO WILL YOU LISTEN TO?

I've found myself looking around lately and wondering, *What in the world is going on?* Recently, my friend's fourth-grade son came home from school with a disappointed look on his face and said,

"Mom, I like girls." My friend responded, "Well, sure! What's wrong with that?" To which her son responded, "Everyone says that's not normal. All my friends are 'they,' bi or gay."

You see, when we step away from whom God says we are, we allow lies to replace truth. Often when we see crazy things happening in the world, we assume it is a fringe movement. We dismiss getting involved, thinking that it could never become mainstream and it won't affect anything. God Himself knows how wrong this thinking is. In fact, history has proven over and over that this mindset is dangerous. Learning from the past can help us in the present and future. As Mark Twain says, "History doesn't repeat itself, but it often rhymes."

I never thought I'd see the day that the most diverse, inclusive country—the United States—would be full of so much hatred. I never thought I'd see the day that I would be judged by the color of my skin or my economic circumstance. The world is upside down, inside out, and sideways. How did this happen?

Isaiah 5:20 says, "Woe to those who call evil good, and good evil; Who substitute darkness for light and light for darkness; Who substitute bitter for sweet and sweet for bitter!"

I see this every single day, whether it's in the grocery store or online. People are calling evil good, and good evil. And God will not stand for it.

Let's reflect for a moment on the history of Nazi Germany. There were likely very few people who believed Hitler was a threat. My heritage is German, so I've traveled to Germany and studied how this could happen. How could good people allow this pure evil to take over their country? I had a difficult time visiting the concentration camps outside Berlin. Can you believe these camps were in neighborhoods of homes? A lie was told about what was really going on, and they dismissed the burning infernos.

The German people were not the only ones trying to reconcile the sweeping evil across the land. The first time I visited Sweden, where my husband is from, I was struck by a blatant display of what's really going on. In the middle of the city center of Gothenburg are three large statues of monkeys displaying "See no evil, hear no evil, speak no evil." These statues show that those who remain neutral end up picking a side against their will. Unfortunately, much of the Church became the "Reich Church" and supported a "Nazified" version of Christianity. Sadly, even today, too many churches submit to the rules of government instead of obeying God. History repeats itself when lessons are not learned.

Now, more than ever, it's important to be grounded in *who you are* because the world will challenge and shame you into believing something you're not. If we fast forward to our current world of technology, we can see that cancel culture is alive and real. Freedom of speech is being censored, causing people to be silent, not speaking or using their voice. I've watched family and friends buckle under the pressure and retreat. The need to avoid conflict keeps people silenced, which is the intention. This is the very behavior that gives the enemy a foothold in our culture: when good people say nothing.

YOU CAN OVERCOME!

So, what is this talk about "the enemy"? Who is he, and why does it matter when thinking about whom God says we are?

The enemy of God is Satan. We learn from Scripture that Satan was an angel who rebelled against God and was cast out of heaven with other fallen angels before the creation of mankind. By tempting Eve to eat the forbidden fruit in the garden, thus causing the fall of mankind. There is now an epic battle between the goodness of God and the evil of Satan, and it is also waging over our souls.

Ephesians 6:12 says, "For our struggle is not against flesh and blood, but against the rulers, against the powers, against the world forces of this darkness, against the spiritual forces of wickedness in the heavenly places."

Currently, Satan's power is over all the nations of the earth until he's dealt with at Jesus's second coming. To learn more about Satan's fate, read Revelation 20. Why is this important? In chapter one, we explored "Who do you think you are?" Know that Satan is the great accuser and wants nothing more than for you to believe the worst about yourself. It's a battle between good and evil. Who are you listening to? You must believe and listen to what God says about you!

It's frightening to think that Satan can influence people in such a way that they are not even aware that they are being tempted toward evil. He affects people's attitudes by lying and giving disinformation. In fact, this is his main objective, to keep you and me apart from our Heavenly Father. There are many words used to describe Satan: tempter, liar, deceiver, and accuser, to name just a few. His deception is one of the most important reasons to be grounded in the truth of who you are in the eyes of God! He'll try to tell you that you're unworthy, that God isn't really good, and you'll need to know what the truth is to combat him! Remember, when you stand for nothing, you fall for anything. Like that rubber duck tossing about in the waves, you need to have a grounded anchor to discern what is true.

Thankfully, part of the truth you can use to anchor yourself is that Satan has no power over you when you are covered by the blood of Jesus! He must get behind you. He has power in this world, but he is already defeated by what Jesus Christ did on the cross. While he influences the world and the people in it now, he is defeated.

Be encouraged and know that you are loved by God and do not have to listen to the lies and accusations of the enemy. Stand your ground and know who you are because of whom *God* says you are. The world's most comprehensive gaslighting campaign is being assaulted against us, and it can make you feel like you're crazy! That is the very purpose of gaslighting; it employs tools such as censorship and propaganda to prop up its effectiveness. The definition of gaslighting is to purposely create confusion and self-doubt. This tactic accuses you of something that has nothing to do with you but distracts and manipulates where the problem lies.

Satan wants to confuse us and keep us from following God's will for our lives. Don't fall for it. It takes courage to stand up against spiritual warfare. At the first sign of conflict, our natural tendency is often "fight-or-flight." Making a choice to stand up and speak out not only keeps your beliefs and actions aligned, but it also sets an example for others to follow. My favorite quote from Billy Graham speaks to this, saying, "Your courage strengthens the spine of others." When you know who you are, you can help other people remind themselves as well!

UNDER CONSTRUCTION

"We are not human beings having a spiritual experience; we are spiritual beings having a human experience."—Pierre Teilhard de Chardin

When we understand that our lives are a journey and our time on planet Earth is just a moment in time, we will live our lives accordingly. We will embrace the understanding that while we are traveling here, we can't do it on our own. Those that try to do otherwise end up empty. Surrendering to God's plan for our lives softens our steps and lightens our load. We don't carry the heavy burden of doing it on our own. We can't rely on our good works nor strive for perfection. We are new creatures in Christ. This is whom Jesus says *we* are.

Aligning how we see ourselves with how God sees us is not a one-and-done proposition. It's something we need to work on continuously. In fact, often, the moment we feel we are in sync, the enemy throws a right punch to knock us off course. That is one of the reasons this re-aligning is a constant practice that can't be ignored. It's like exercising a muscle that will strengthen your core. When exercised consistently, you will discover an inner peace that surpasses all understanding.

It's taken me most of my life to realize that I am indefinitely under construction. At one point, I thought I had done the work and settled back into life. I was coasting along and wasn't addressing or concerning myself with who I was. I got lost and allowed fear and what other people wanted me to be to control me. This created unresolved resentments that started showing up physically, even as spurts of rage. I started having panic attacks and lived with a nagging sense of hopelessness.

Those paralyzing moments were the catalysts I needed to hook back up to the anchor.

At the time, I was remarried and welcomed beautiful twin daughters into my life. I was now a mother of five children, and ending a marriage was non-negotiable in my book. However, when my marriage inevitably fell apart, it opened my eyes to how deeply connected our choices are with our identity. Though I justified that I could just hang on and put on a fake smile since everything else was working in my life, I needed a come-to-Jesus moment about the choices that I had made that were not in line with Scripture. I quickly discovered that when our life is not congruent with our identity in Jesus, it comes out one way or another, whether physically or emotionally. This was a season in my life where I drifted. I know that God never left me, but I took things for granted until I had a wake-up call. It's true that when you hit rock bottom, it causes you to look up.

Remember, shame over your past doesn't define you. We all make bad decisions or slip up. This Scripture brings the reality to bear that the old really is gone!

"Therefore if anyone is in Christ, this person is a new creation; the old things passed away; behold, new things have come." (2 Corinthians 5:17)

One of the ways to stay anchored to truth and remember your true identity is to create a habit of connecting with God consistently. Whether you must set a timer or make an appointment in your calendar, make this your top priority above all else. I promise from my own experience that you can't let this priority slip—you will ultimately drift away from the truth as human nature takes over. It takes discipline to stay on course and live in the truth, but it is possible. It's helpful to surround yourself with people and activities that support your goals.

One of the things my husband and I do each morning is start our day with devotions and prayer. Often, it's difficult to quiet the mind. A friend shared this four-step process with me that I hope is helpful for you:

1. Quiet the Soul

Find a peaceful place where you won't be disturbed. I have a favorite big white oversized chair in the corner of our bedroom, surrounded by stacks of books, paper, and pens. Settle in, close your eyes, and take a few breaths. Try to quiet the racing thoughts in your mind and be present with Jesus.

2. Read Scripture

There are many ways to create structure for reading the Bible, which we'll discuss in a later chapter. However, the most important thing is to simply open it every day. I love randomly flipping through my Bible because every word has meaning and is helpful. Often the page will land right where I need it most!

3. Talk to God and Pray

Ask Him what He wants to reveal through the Scriptures. Praise Him and thank Him. Tell Him about your day and your concerns. God has the best success strategies, so ask Him!

4. Listen and Hear from Him

This is the tough part. It's easy for us to talk and list off everything in our minds, but God wants to talk to you, too! Now it's your turn to listen. Be still and know that He is God. What is He telling you?

Another tip that will help you stay in connection with God is to create surroundings that bring you a sanctuary of peace. For example, we recently built a new home and purposely created a space that reflects our goals. If you walk through our home, you will feel the presence of the Lord from the décor to the sound system playing worship music. The spirit of the Lord is in this place!

* * *

Now it's time for you to reflect on what we've talked about throughout this chapter—do you feel like a rubber ducky? Or are you anchored to the truth? Maybe you're somewhere in between. Wherever you're at, God wants to solidify your identity before moving on. Take some time to journal who you think you are as it aligns with who God says you are. What changes can you make? Pray and ask God to guide you. In addition, be thinking about seeking out mentors that are aligned with your goals. We will be exploring this more as we continue.

Water Walker Reflections:

*Journal some examples where you felt like that rubber ducky in the storms of life: _____

_____

_____

_____

_____

*Knowing you can now choose to tether yourself to the anchor of God, reflect on how you can choose to do so: ____

_____

_____

_____

_____

_____

What storm are you currently going through? What are some things you can do to stay tethered to God's anchor?

_____

_____

_____

_____

_____

*Whose voices have you been listening to about who you are? The opinions of family members or friends? Satan? God?_____

_____

_____

_____

_____

*How can you tune in to the voice of God speaking about who you are? _____

_____

_____

_____

_____

*Write down who you are as God sees you:_____

_____

_____

_____

_____

*Describe your "white room" experience with God (and if you haven't done the exercise yet, do it now!) _____

_____

_____

_____

_____

*Make a plan for your daily time with God: _____

_____

_____

_____

_____

Ripple Effect:

*How will adjusting the way you see yourself and aligning it with God's Word impact your life? _____

_____

_____

_____

_____

*How will the way you see yourself as God sees you influence and be an inspiration to others? _____

_____

_____

_____

_____

Chapter 3

WHO DO YOU THINK JESUS IS?

> "You have made us for yourself, O Lord, and our hearts are restless until they rest in you."
>
> —St. Augustine of Hippo

IN 1670, BLAISE Pascal penned, "There is a God-shaped vacuum in the heart of every man which cannot be filled by any created thing, but only by God the Creator, made known through Jesus Christ."

Whether or not we are aware of it, we are all on a lifelong search for meaning and purpose. God's answer for our searching is His Son, Jesus, yet most worldly paths lead people *away* from Jesus. So, dear reader, I'll ask you an important question: How much thought and research have you done to really *know* who Jesus is?

I recently watched a series of "People on the Street" interviews wherein passersby were asked, "Who is Jesus?" Most people answered that yes, he probably was a real person. However, they believed he was simply a teacher, a prophet, or someone who taught others how to be a good person, like Gandhi and Muhammad. When they were then asked if Jesus was the Messiah, the Son of God, almost everybody said, "No, that is just a story." Several went on to say that they believed that religion was the source of most wars over centuries, so, overall, "Religion is a bad thing."

Therein lies the problem. Many people are confused by what Christianity is, but they are even more confused as to what it means for us. To clarify this great confusion, Christianity is unique because it is less about involving humanity's attempt to reach God, but rather more about God's attempt to reach humanity. Unlike other religions, it's not up to us to clean ourselves up or be a good enough person to gain the approval we're looking for. Jesus did the unthinkable for us—while we were still sinners, He died for us and gave us a clean slate, making a way for us to live with Him forever. What other god paid the price for us to be fully free? What other god created the entire Universe with His words? (Hint: The answer is none. Only Jesus.)

"So Paul stood in the midst of the Areopagus and said: "Men of Athens, I see that you are very religious in all respects. For while I was passing through and examining the objects of your worship, I also found an altar with this inscription,

'TO AN UNKNOWN GOD.' Therefore, what you worship in ignorance, this I proclaim to you. The God who made the world and everything that is in it, since He is Lord of heaven and earth, does not dwell in temples made by hands; nor is He served by human hands, as though He needed anything, since He Himself gives to all people life and breath and all things; and He made from one man every nation of mankind to live on all the face of the earth, having determined their appointed times and the boundaries of their habitation, that they would seek God, if perhaps they might feel around for Him and find Him, though He is not far from each one of us." (Acts 17:22-27)

These words from Paul are just as powerful today, and I'll bet if he were still around, he'd say the same thing on the streets while those interviews were being conducted. We need more modern-day Pauls on the street to set the record straight. In today's world, we tend to compartmentalize our views, thinking that talking about Jesus should be relegated to attending church on Sunday.

However, before I understood who Jesus *really* is, I probably would have answered the interviewer on the street the same way. When I was growing up, I attended Catholic grade school. We would begin each day with a long walk down a narrow hallway that led to the church sanctuary. I didn't like the smells or the unnerving, heavy robes the priests wore. I couldn't understand a single word during the hour-long sermon because the priests all spoke Latin.

We weren't given Bibles, but instead were offered confusing catechisms, rosaries, and the ever-present, looming closet with a curtain known as the confessional. A confessional is a box, cabinet, booth, or stall in which the priest in Catholic churches sits to hear the confessions of penitents.

We entered through the curtain individually, knelt, then spoke through another curtain with a man on the other side. Each time, I was petrified with anxiety at this terrifying process that I did not understand. Imagine being a child asked to go into a dark confessional and talk to a priest you couldn't see! Thankfully, I would later learn in my own search that we have direct access to our Heavenly Father. The concept of confession of sin to a priest is not taught in Scripture.

In the Old Testament, the people needed a priest to intercede between them and God. Now, we can approach God directly, without the use of a human mediator. Why? Because Jesus Christ is our great High Priest. In that horrible moment when Jesus died on the cross, the Gospels tell us the thick veil (or curtain) that separated the Holy Place from the Most Holy Place in the Temple was torn in two from top to bottom.

"And behold, the veil of the temple was torn in two from top to bottom; and the earth shook and the rocks were split." (Matthew 27:51)

When the veil was torn, that which kept man from God's presence was completely removed.

In the Catholic classroom, I was traumatized by the teachers who were robe-clothed nuns. I can't remember how many times I was bopped on the head with a pointer stick by them—a common practice to "get our attention." Between the classroom and confessional, my religious childhood caused me to eventually turn away from God because nothing about it felt loving. Looking back, I can see why people have negative beliefs and feelings toward Christianity because I was in that category as well.

WHAT WOULD JESUS DO?

I love discussing and learning about people and their beliefs. I often hear similar stories of disappointment from religious experiences, and I feel it's important to have those conversations.

This always gets me thinking about how people would respond if they met Jesus Himself.

In Scripture, we find a surprising contrast in how Jesus interacted with his fellow Jews, disciples and Pharisees (the religious leaders), and those of other religions. Obviously, Jesus' ministry was mainly in regions represented by Jews, yet he found opportunities to interact with foreigners of different beliefs. The Gospels reveal Jesus spoke with Romans, who came from a polytheistic background; with Syrians and Canaanites, traditionally worshippers of idols including Baal and Ashtoreth; and with Samaritans, whose religion was similar to Judaism. In Luke 7, Jesus interacts with a Roman centurion and heals his sick servant; in Luke 10, we find Him with the good Samaritan; and in Luke 17, He heals the Samaritan leper. Jesus also interacts with a Canaanite woman with a sick daughter in Matthew 15, the Roman governor Pilate in John 18-19, and a sinful Samaritan woman at a well in John 4.

It's what Jesus *did* and *did not do* during these interactions that we can learn from.

What Jesus did:

- He LOVED them
- He healed the sick
- He delivered them from demonic oppression
- He invited them to turn from their sin and follow Him

- He told them to tell others what God has done for them

What Jesus did not do:

- Condemn or rebuke
- Debate and argue

How would the survey on the street compare if Christians wholeheartedly followed Jesus' example? Let's take this to heart and truly be like Jesus. There's a popular acronym called WWJD: "What Would Jesus Do?" But do we really think about what He would do in our everyday interactions? In John 13:35, it says that the world will know we are Christians by the way we love one another. Can this be said of us?

IT'S NOT ABOUT GOOD WORKS!

"Thomas said to Him, 'Lord, we do not know where You are going; how do we know the way?' Jesus said to him, 'I am the way, and the truth, and the life; no one comes to the Father except through Me.'" (John 14:5-6)

All roads to eternal life go through Jesus. God said it, yet man wants to have many roads to Heaven—and God Himself. This makes many people uncomfortable because they want to have many roads to reconciliation. However, it's clearly stated in the Bible that the road is narrow, and the only way to Heaven is through Jesus.

Matthew 7:13-14 says, "Enter through the narrow gate; for the gate is wide and the way is broad that leads to destruction, and there are many who enter through it. For the gate is narrow and the way is constricted that leads to life, and there are few who find it."

Often when people are asked if they think they will go to Heaven when they die, they will answer, "yes." When asked why, the most common answer is, "Because I'm a good person."

That couldn't be further from the truth. We can't get to Heaven by good works or trying to avoid sin and live a perfect life. No one could ever live up to the standard of being perfect—that's why the Old Testament is so beautiful. Before Jesus came to earth to die in our place and rise again, the law was rigorous and required sacrifices and rituals to even come close to God's presence. But now we live in the *new* covenant, where Jesus made a way for us. And it is only by His grace that we can live as sons and daughters, guaranteed eternal life with Him.

Ephesians 2:8-9 says, "For by grace you have been saved through faith; and this is not of yourselves, it is the gift of God; not a result of works, so that no one may boast."

This invitation is for *everyone*; Jesus knocks on our heart's door, but we must respond and invite him in.

"Behold, I stand at the door and knock; if anyone hears My voice and opens the door, I will come in to him and will dine with him, and he with Me." (Revelation 3:20)

WHAT DO OTHER PEOPLE BELIEVE?

In 2020, I started hosting a weekly Zoom Bible Study. It's been deeply rewarding to study Scripture with a group of women as we learn, grow, and encourage each other. Over a recent Christmas holiday, we added a 4-week series where invited guests were encouraged to "Discover Christ in Christmas." Each week, we featured a guest speaker who shared their testimony about how they found Jesus.

The first guest was Pastor Bijay Kumar Dahal, a former Nepalese Buddhist, who shared his story about a teenager from Campus Crusade of Christ witnessing to him about Jesus. He was brought to tears as he realized the saving grace of Jesus was what he was searching for, and all it took was a young teenager's witness!

What do Buddhists believe about Jesus? In 2001, the Dalai Lama stated, "Jesus Christ reached a high state as an enlightened person."

Our second week featured my friend Jerry Roisentul, who was raised Jewish and has an incredible story of discovering that Jesus is the Messiah. He was on the floor of his apartment getting ready to take his own life. God miraculously spared his life, and the very next week, he went to a church and gave his life to Christ.

Our Jewish brothers and sisters are aligned with our belief in the Heavenly Father; however, they do not accept that Jesus is the Messiah and are still waiting for Him to come. Many of my Jewish friends have now given their lives to Jesus, and they are known as Messianic Jews.

What do traditional Jews believe about Jesus? Judaism gave birth to Christianity, and the Old Testament (Tanakh) contained prophecies about the coming Messiah. Jews believe Jesus did not fulfill messianic prophecies that establish the criteria for the coming of the Messiah. Judaism does not accept Jesus as a divine being, an intermediary between humans and God, a Messiah, or holy.

Our third week featured my friend Katherine Lutz, who was raised in a very strict Atheist home. Katherine heard the Gospel for the first time at the age of 28 and immediately asked Jesus into her heart to be her personal Lord and Savior. As she began to read the Bible, she found peace in understanding the meaning and purpose of life. God was the missing piece to her puzzle, and it changed everything. Today, she mentors thousands of women, not only in her business but also (and more importantly) in her faith!

What do Atheists believe about Jesus? While all Atheists believe there is no God, some believe Jesus was an actual person who lived, but that He certainly was not God or a Savior. They often believe He is a myth like the "telephone" game—passed down through so many different sources that the original message was completely lost.

Our fourth week featured former Muslim Abdul Coly from Michigan, who had an incredible story that started with a breakup. He was crushed because his Christian girlfriend ended the relationship with him because he did not believe in Jesus. As he prayed for guidance, he literally had an encounter with Jesus!

What do Muslims (followers of Islam) believe about Jesus? According to Vox Magazine, "Muslims believe that Jesus (called "Isa" in Arabic) was a prophet of God and was born to a virgin (Mary). They also believe he will return to Earth before the Day of Judgment to restore justice and defeat al-Masih ad-Dajjal, or "the false messiah"—also known as the Antichrist. So, although Muslims do not believe that Jesus is the son of God—a critically important distinction between Muslim and Christian views of him—Muslims do revere Jesus as an important prophet."

Other beliefs such as Deism, Hinduism, Polytheism, and Agnosticism have diverse views, but none accept Jesus as the Messiah. Messiah is the promised deliverer of the Jewish nation prophesied in the Hebrew Bible. Messiah Jesus is a core tenant of Christianity because He fulfilled the prophecies of the Old Testament (Hebrew Bible).

Deists believe in the existence of a supreme being, our Creator God, but that God does not intervene in the Universe. It's an intellectual movement that accepts the existence of a creator on the basis of reason but rejects belief in a supernatural deity who interacts with humankind.

Hindus are more than willing to acknowledge Jesus as divine if He is not seen as *uniquely* divine. Hindus often worship many gods and goddesses, and some are eager to include Jesus on their list of deities. They don't, however, see Jesus as the only way to God. Instead, some understand Jesus as the perfect example of *self-realization* (the goal of Hindu *dharma*).

Polytheists believe in more than one god. The ancient Greeks, for example, were polytheists; their gods included Apollo, Athena, Dionysus, and Zeus.

An ***Agnostic*** is a person who believes that nothing is known or can be known of the existence or nature of God, or of anything beyond material phenomena; a person who claims neither faith nor disbelief in God.

Since I have close friends and ties with Jamaica as a former owner of a resort there, I wanted to include ***Rastafarism***. I love the Jamaican people. Rastafarism is a movement (religious and cultural) that started in Jamaica in the 1930s. Contrary to popular belief, likely because of Bob Marley, Rasta isn't just a reflection of the particularly catchy genre of music called Reggae!

Rastas believe that Jesus is an important figure in Rastafari. However, practitioners reject the traditional Christian view of Jesus, particularly the depiction of Him as a white European, believing that this is a perversion of the truth. They believe that Jesus was a black African, and that the white Jesus was a false god. Their God is black Jah. They also believe in reincarnation.

The ***New Age*** movement is one of the most misunderstood belief systems, and operates under the idea that "we are God." New Age affirms the belief in the divinity of each individual. New Agers are united in their rejection of traditional monotheism (belief in one all-powerful God). Instead, they embrace Monism, the belief that everything is one, and pantheism, the belief that God is everything. In fact, when it comes to God, New Agers believe that the "self is the seat of the divine." That is, there is a god-aspect within each of us, a tiny sliver of god in every person. A New Ager will believe Jesus was a good person, teacher, or prophet, but not the pathway to heaven. Yoga is an introduction pathway to Hinduism, posing to deities and meditating to Buddha. I stretch to revitalize the health of my mind, body and spirit, but I call my mat a "fitness mat." Fortune tellers, crystals and tarot cards are part of the occult.

These are just a few of thousands of religions and world-views that do not believe God's word that Jesus is the Messiah. It is obvious that Satan has been very busy distracting and con-fusing us, as I mentioned in the previous chapter. Do not be deceived. Seek and search for the truth. While we all "co-exist," as the well-known bumper sticker suggests, there is only one who reconciles us with God, and it is Jesus.

LIGHT VS. DARKNESS

Satan has a way of subtly altering things just enough to mimic the one and only salvation plan through Jesus Christ alone. For instance, when we become born again by repenting and accepting Jesus as our Savior, we are given the Holy Spirit. The Christian "God within" is the Holy Spirit, part of the Trinity: God, Jesus, and the Holy Spirit. Many believe by our own good works and evolution, the "god within" is us. A typical reference is "the god or goddess within," evolving into a human state of "god" without Christ's intervention.

You cannot earn your deity. That is a cult. Satan and his army of demons know this, and they can mimic Holy Spirit with the occult.

Astrology is just one facet of how New Age is hijacking the beauty of God's creation through astronomy. There's a fascinating book first published in 1882 featuring a series of lectures by Joseph A. Seiss called *The Gospel in The Stars*. The constellations tell the story of the battle between the Serpent (Satan) and the Cross, with the Cross being "Christ" the victor.

Seiss writes, "New Age has perverted God's sacred, divine science based on superstition which Astrology has prostituted to its own end. It is our duty to search out and turn it to its proper evangelical use."

Before doing my own research and finding Seiss's book, I was often confronted with the question: "What do you think of astrology?" Because I was always curious about the stars and their meaning, I answered, "I'm not sure, but I know someone who does!" (Of course, that someone would be our Heavenly Father.) Seeking to learn more led me to the realization that God reveals Himself through Scripture *and* through His creation. His glory and beauty can be found in the splendor of nature and in the skies and the stars.

Romans 1:20 says, "For since the creation of the world His invisible *attributes, that is,* His eternal power and divine nature, have been clearly perceived, being understood by what has been made, so that they are without excuse."

WHO DO I THINK JESUS IS?

As I shared in Chapter 1, my early feelings around God were quite traumatizing, so I didn't even give it much thought. I didn't attend church other than a wedding or funeral. I just focused on my life with the day-to-day cares and concerns. It wasn't until I was pregnant with my first child that I became curious about life and the pure joy, awe, and wonder of a baby growing inside me. I pondered a lot about life, my role as a parent, and the responsibility of raising a family.

At that same time, my upline, Julie, who sponsored me into my first direct sales company, invited me to a Bible study. Julie was a woman that radiated something special that I couldn't quite understand, and I had always admired that about her. Needless to say, I was curious to learn more and accepted her invitation. I came to learn that what radiated from Julie and the other women in the Bible study was the Holy Spirit, and I wanted that in my life!

I eventually learned about what Jesus had done for me and the beauty of a life with Him, and it was at that study that I invited Him into my heart. A story that fascinated me immediately was in John 1 when Nathaniel was sitting under the fig tree and Jesus told him that He knew him even before they ever met.

"Jesus saw Nathanael coming to Him, and said of him, 'Here is truly an Israelite, in whom there is no deceit!' Nathanael said to Him, 'How do You know me?' Jesus answered and said to him, 'Before Philip called you, when you were under the fig tree, I saw you.' Nathanael answered Him, 'Rabbi, You are the Son of God; You are the King of Israel!' Jesus answered and said to him, 'Because I said to you that I saw you under the fig tree, do you believe? You will see greater things than these.'" (John 1: 47-50)

To fathom that kind of love—a love that knew of us before we were ever conceived—was something I wanted. So, shortly before my son was born, I changed his name to Nathaniel, rather than Bradley, as a reminder of my newfound faith.

WHAT DO YOU BELIEVE?
AND WHY DOES IT MATTER?

It matters who *you* think Jesus is. He wasn't just a teacher, a good man, or a prophet. He is the Son of God. I encourage you to give this some thought and journal about what it is that you believe. Often people will study their fantasy football lineup more than they ponder what they actually believe about life, death, and their destiny for eternity.

So, who do *you* think Jesus is?

We will all have to answer the most important question: "Where do you think you will go when you die?" As I shared, the most common answers to this question are, "I am a good person, so I will go to Heaven," or, "Well, my parents baptized me as a baby, so I'm good." I've also heard people say, "Yeah, I pretty much messed up my life, so I'll probably go to Hell." This is heartbreaking because Jesus offers salvation freely to everyone, no matter how messed up we are! The enemy wants you to believe that you are beyond hope. Remember Jesus' final words to the thief crucified next to Him on the cross:

"And He said to him, 'Truly I say to you, today you will be with Me in Paradise.'" (Luke 23:43)

My motivation for writing this book is to help spread the word that no matter what we've done, God is knocking at our heart's door wanting to be invited in. Will you open it up and let Him in?

Matthew 7:7-8 says, "Ask, and it will be given to you; seek, and you will find; knock, and it will be opened to you. For everyone who asks receives, and the one who seeks finds, and to the one who knocks it will be opened."

Water Walker Reflection:

What are your current beliefs about Jesus and who He is?

_____
_____
_____
_____
_____

What or who has influenced you to believe this?

_____
_____
_____
_____
_____

Ripple Effect:

Journal your thoughts as to how your beliefs have influenced others: _____

_____
_____
_____
_____
_____

Chapter 4

WHO GOD SAYS JESUS IS

NOW THAT WE'VE explored who *we* think Jesus is, let's look at what the Bible (the Word of God) says Jesus is. Jesus is more than a teacher, prophet, or mentor, but before we delve into who *God* says Jesus is, we need to get a basic understanding of what we know as the Trinity: Father, Son, and the Holy Spirit. These are not simply names for different *parts* of God but rather the collective names for the three persons who exist in God as a single entity. They—Father, Son, and Holy Spirit—cannot be separate from one another. Each person is understood as having an identical essence or nature, not merely similar natures. There is only one God, and He exists as the Trinity. The Father is God, the Son is God, and the Holy Spirit is God; they are not three gods but one. The Father is not the

Son, the Son is not the Spirit, and the Spirit is not the Father. Each is God individually, and yet they exist together as the one true God of the Bible. So, instead of asking who God says Jesus is, perhaps we should ask, "Who does the Bible say Jesus is?"

Well, a good place to start is in Genesis 1:1-2: "In the beginning God created the heavens and the earth. And the earth was a formless and desolate emptiness, and darkness was over the surface of the deep, and the Spirit of God was hovering over the surface of the waters."

Here we see that God, the Father and the Son, create together, and the Holy Spirit is hovering over the waters. Later, in Genesis 1:26, God uses a very specific pronoun: "Then God said, 'Let Us make mankind in Our image, according to Our likeness.'"

God existed in community from the very beginning, Father, Son, and Holy Spirit together! All throughout scripture, we can find evidence of this same pronoun being used. How cool is that?!

John 10:30 also says, "I and the Father are one."

The Trinity is a core tenet of the Christian faith. In fact, not believing in it has created sects, such as Jehovah's Witnesses. Jehovah's Witnesses was formed in the late 1800s from a Bible study in Pennsylvania. They strayed from Christian doctrine by believing that the Heavenly Father is the *only* God, and not Jesus or Holy Spirit—in addition to many other extrabiblical beliefs. These slight shifts may seem irrelevant, but we are cautioned not to stray from the Word of God to create new doctrine.

THE DIVINE CROSS REFERENCE

Now that we know *who* Jesus is, let's explore *why* this is important. As a child, I visited Yellowstone National Park. One of the highlights for me was observing the Old Faithful geyser. According to Merriam-Webster, "A geyser is a rare kind of hot spring that is under pressure and erupts, sending jets of water and steam into the air." But where does it come from? What we don't see is what's happening under the Earth to cause it. Geysers happen out of our line of sight. They result from the heating of groundwater by shallow bodies of magma. And so it is for you and me! What is happening on the outside will flow out of what's on the inside. Our "magma," in this case, is our belief system from which our choices and actions spring forth.

So, what is your belief system? Does it line up with who Jesus really is?

To answer these questions, we must understand who the Bible says Jesus is!

First, we must understand that Jesus was prophesied throughout the Old Testament. He was the fulfillment of the words spoken to generations upon generations before His coming to Earth. You can trace this throughout the Bible, seeing the confirmation of Old Testament scriptures in the New Testament. I call this God's divine cross reference for those like doubting Thomas who want proof! Thomas the Apostle wasn't present when Jesus appeared to the disciples in the upper room after His resurrection. Thus, he doubted Jesus until Jesus showed him the nail marks in His hands.

John 20:25-29 says, "So the other disciples were saying to him, 'We have seen the Lord!' But he said to them, 'Unless I see in His hands the imprint of the nails, and put my finger into the place of the nails, and put my hand into His side, I will not believe.' Eight days later His disciples were again inside, and Thomas was with them. Jesus came, the doors having been shut, and stood in their midst and said, 'Peace be to you.' Then He said to Thomas, 'Place your finger here, and see My hands; and take your hand and put it into My side; and do not continue in disbelief, but be a believer.' Thomas answered and said to Him, 'My Lord and my God!' Jesus said to him, 'Because you have seen Me, have you now believed? Blessed are they who did not see, and yet believed.'"

I am constantly fascinated by the Word of God. There are hundreds of cross-references between the Old and New Testaments, as seen in this photo:

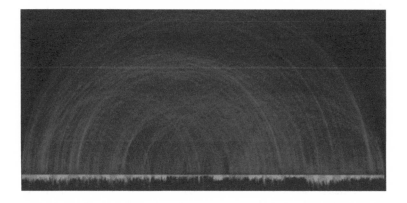

The bottom of this chart is all the verses of the Bible, and the lines on the chart show all the times a specific verse referred to a different verse. How beautiful is that image? What else in creation is tied together so uniformly from beginning to end?

One of the major prophecies of the Old Testament is about the coming of the Messiah. The Old Testament says the Messiah would come from the house of King David (2 Samuel); would be born of a virgin (Isaiah); would be born in Bethlehem (Micah); and would end up in Egypt for a time (Hosea). Of course, all these prophecies were fulfilled by Jesus! His genealogy traced back to King David; He was born of the virgin Mary in Bethlehem; and the holy family had to flee to Egypt to escape the persecution of King Herod shortly after Jesus's birth.

Psalm 22 predicts that the Messiah would be forsaken and scorned with His hands and feet pierced and His clothing gambled, and this is confirmed again in Matthew 27:35: "And when they had crucified Him, they divided His garments among themselves by casting lots."

The plot to kill God's anointed one is prophesied in Psalm 31 and Psalm 38 that the Messiah will be silent before His accusers.

Some of the most important Old Testament prophecies about Jesus are also confirmed in the New Testament concerning His death and resurrection. The anointed one would be the Passover Lamb, whose blood over the door saved the people of Israel from death in Egypt and whose bones were not to be broken (Exodus). Jesus is called the Passover Lamb by Paul in 1 Corinthians, and the Gospel of John shows how Jesus's bones were not broken during his crucifixion, as was the common practice at the time.

The Bible also reveals how *we*, the believers—also referred to as the Church—are supposed to live. Many confuse the word *church* (the building) with the intended use of *Church* as the collective noun referring to the followers of the Christian faith; not unlike our earlier discussion about the term *temple*, which is actually inside of us—*we* are the Church.

SURPRISED BY JESUS

Of course, the Bible is the number one source for evidence of who Jesus really is. In addition, there are thousands of documented archaeological discoveries proving the accuracy of the Bible. To name just a few, Noah's Ark, the parting of the Red Sea, the Tower of Babel, and the Shroud of Turin can all be proven as fact. A couple of good places to start delving into this are online at www.museumofthebible.org and www.answersingenesis.org

There are many people who made it their priority to seek out evidence regarding the Bible's claims about who Jesus is. One of them is Lee Strobel, an award-winning investigative reporter and legal editor at the *Chicago Tribune*. Lee was a devout atheist whose wife, Leslie, suddenly became a Christian. This led Lee to utilize his journalistic and legal training to try and invalidate the claims of Jesus. Determined to prove his wife wrong, he delved head-first into this journey. However, his overwhelming research confirmed that what the Bible said about Jesus was, in fact, true! Their story led to the book (and now movie) "The Case for Christ."

Another favorite example of mine is author C. S. Lewis, who was raised as an Atheist. While at school, his friendship with fellow intellectuals who were Christians, including J.R.R. Tolkien and Hugo Dyson, led to countless debates and discussions. They challenged him to consider the logical, mythological, and literary cases for Christianity. These conversations and research eventually led to him giving his life to Jesus! The 2021 movie "The Most Reluctant Convert" chronicles this journey as he went on to write books like "The Chronicles of Narnia," "Mere Christianity," and "Surprised by Joy."

I believe this is a lost art: having conversations and healthy, loving debates to explore the meaning of life. Wouldn't you like to be surprised by joy? Consider that what God says about Jesus is true!

EASTER ISN'T JUST A HOLIDAY

The more I walk with Jesus in my faith, the more I am humbled and fascinated by His courage. He knew His fate! Everyone loves Christmas, as do I. We know this was just one fulfilled prophecy of Him descending to Earth through a virgin birth. Consider the burden of knowing that His Father sent *Him*, His only son, to pay the price for our sins.

One of my favorite teaching pastors is Jack Hibbs of Calvary Chapel in Chino Hills, California. When my husband, Thomas, and I are in California, we drive to attend his church. In a recent Palm Sunday message, Jack described in great detail the anguish Jesus felt entering the gates on the donkey. Think of that! As everyone was praising and laying palms at his feet, Jesus *wept.*

Luke 19:41 says, "When He approached Jerusalem, He saw the city and wept over it."

I couldn't help but cry at the thought. Why was Jesus weeping? He knew what was about to happen to him, yet he wept for they did not know His fate.

Good Friday—the day that Jesus went to the cross—was *not* a good day for Him. It was a good day for us, as our sins were nailed with Him on the cross, but it was a horrific day for Jesus. When he prayed in the garden the night before he was crucified, he was literally sweating blood. Hematidrosis is a very rare condition in which an individual sweats blood when they are suffering from extreme levels of stress. Do you have a child? Can you imagine how you would want to rescue your child from this pain? I can't even imagine. This was anguish for not only Jesus, but His Father as well. Who would take his place? Jesus had the entire burden of the world on His shoulders.

Luke 22:42-44 says, "'Father, if You are willing, remove this cup from Me; yet not My will, but Yours be done.' Now an angel from heaven appeared to Him, strengthening Him. And being in agony, He was praying very fervently; and His sweat became like drops of blood, falling down upon the ground."

This wasn't the only time the enemy tempted Jesus to walk away from His calling. Imagine that! Just like us, the enemy continuously tries to disrupt God's plan for Jesus.

"Then Jesus was led up by the Spirit into the wilderness to be tempted by the devil. And after He had fasted for forty days and forty nights, He then became hungry. And the tempter came and said to Him, 'If You are the Son of God, command that these stones become bread.' But He answered and said, 'It is written: "Man shall not live on bread alone, but on every word that comes out of the mouth of God."' Then the devil took Him along into the holy city and had Him stand on the pinnacle of the temple, and he said to Him, 'If You are the Son of God, throw Yourself down; for it is written: "He will give His angels orders concerning You"; and "On their hands they will lift You up, So that You do not strike Your foot against a stone.'" Jesus said to him, 'On the other hand, it is written: "You shall not put the Lord your God to the test.'" Again, the devil took Him along to a very high mountain and showed Him all the kingdoms of the world and their glory; and he said to Him, 'All these things I will give You, if You fall down and worship me.' Then Jesus said to him, 'Go away, Satan! For it is written: "You shall worship the Lord your God, and serve Him only.'"" (Matthew 4:1-10)

Remember that line when YOU are under attack:

"Away from me, Satan!"

Had Jesus not gone to the cross, there would be no Easter Sunday. There would be no reason to celebrate! For many have proclaimed to be God, but Jesus is the only one who raised from the dead—just like He said He would.

Easter is not just a *story*; it is the Good News that God fulfilled His promises to us.

My friend Chris Widener, speaker and bestselling author of "Four Seasons," shared a profound statement about Easter:

"The problem with Easter is that it can never be just a nice day. It can never be just a day for family, food and traditions. It is more than that. Easter is actually a day that confronts us with a decision about the greatest claim ever made in human history.

Easter is only one of two things. It hinges on the claim that Jesus Christ was God in human flesh and was raised from the dead. So that means that Easter is either the greatest hoax ever perpetrated upon mankind or it is the single-most important event in human history.

"If Jesus did not come back to life and ascend into heaven, then billions of people have bought into a total lie.

"However, if Jesus Christ really was raised from the dead, it means that His claims were true, and it brings every human being who ever lived to a point of decision. If His resurrection is true, then it means His claims and teachings were true as well. It means that He really was God's messenger to Earth.

"Everyone is confronted with the reality that they must make a decision about that singular event. Is the story of Jesus a fraud, or is it true? Those are really the only two options because it either happened or it didn't. No one else can make that decision for you.

"I would say that since the stakes are so high, it requires that every human being at least research and come to a decision for themselves. Most people will spend more time researching a vacation than spending the time to research these claims.

"Modern man will tell you that smart people don't believe the so-called myth of Jesus, but even today—and throughout history—some of the smartest people in the world believe that Jesus really did walk the earth, was killed, and then rose from the dead."

THINK ETERNITY!

Over a year ago, God was nudging me to start a Bible study. I shrugged it off for months and made tons of excuses. He practically had to wrestle me down for my attention! However, I know by now that when we center ourselves in the will of God, it comes with ease and blessings. Well, I was finally obedient, and now some of my favorite days are Wednesdays spent with our beautiful Zoom Bible study community!

The morning of the first Bible study, I woke up at about 4 a.m. I was nervous, but I started praying. As I sat with Him and listened, God kept saying two words to me: "Think eternity."

What God? I uttered, almost under my breath.

"Think eternity."

But God, the Bible study is called, "I Do Hard Things." I don't understand.

Again, He said to me, "Think eternity."

Before I had time to try to digest what was happening, He said, "Fishers of men." Then I realized what He was communicating to me. He wanted me to know what was most important to *Him*. All the nervous thoughts and emotions I was feeling to effectively lead a Bible study suddenly melted to a peaceful understanding of two simple words: Think eternity. I knew that if I took my mind off of what I needed to do and say and allowed *Him* to do the work, to flow through me, I would be operating in His will. I would be thinking about eternal things.

"And He said to them, 'Follow Me, and I will make you fishers of people.'" (Matthew 4:19)

Above all else, He wants us to think about our eternal life, and to have as many come with us as possible. We must be fishers of men (and women!).

What would happen to our priorities if we focused on these two words: *Think eternity*? Why does eternity matter to you? This is a question you have to ask yourself before we move forward. Are you "thinking eternity"?

THE GIFT OF ETERNAL LIFE

As I hope you can see by now, the study of Scripture reveals who God says Jesus is. Jesus is alive! He is not a story or myth. He is real. What pure joy and hope this should bring you!

He not only walked on water, but He was also born from a virgin birth, descending to Earth to save us. He took our place on the cross to pay the penalty for our sins. He was resurrected from the dead. For 40 days, He showed the world what His resurrection truly meant. He was seen by thousands in His restored body, and after those 40 days, He ascended into Heaven to prepare a home for us. Ten days later (fifty days after His resurrection), the Holy Spirit descended on the disciples to complete the work, and now He lives in us! This same Holy Spirit is available to you when you repent and ask Jesus into your heart as your Savior.

So, dear reader, have you invited Him into your heart? The Bible reads:

"For all have sinned and come short of the glory of God." (Romans 3:23)

"For the wages of sin is death, but the gift of God is eternal life through Jesus Christ our Lord." (Hebrews 9:27)

"For whosoever shall call upon the name of the Lord shall be saved." (Romans 6:23)

YOU are a whosoever. And you have a choice to accept this invitation. Will you?

If you would like to receive the gift of salvation that God has for you today, I want you to say these words—out loud!

Dear Lord Jesus, come into my heart. Forgive me of my sin. Wash me and cleanse me. Set me free. Jesus, thank you for dying for me. I believe that You are risen from the dead and that You're coming back again. Fill me with the Holy Spirit. Give me a passion for the lost, a hunger for the things of God, and a holy boldness to preach the gospel of Jesus Christ. I'm saved, I'm born again, I'm forgiven, and I'm on my way to Heaven because I have Jesus in my heart.

If you just prayed those words for the first time, as a believer of the gospel of Jesus Christ, I tell you today that *all* of your sins are forgiven through Jesus! I am so happy for you and am excited to meet and know you and greet you as we live in Heaven for eternity!

Water Walker Reflections:

After reading what Scripture has to say about who Jesus is, reflect on how this impacts your own beliefs:

_____

_____

_____

_____

_____

Reflect and consider the price Jesus paid for us. Allow this thought to really wash over you. Do you know how much He loves you? _____

_____

_____

_____

_____

Is there anything holding you back from surrendering to the gift of salvation through Jesus Christ? _____

_____

_____

_____

_____

What are your thoughts as you "think eternity"? _____

_____

_____

_____

_____

Ripple Effect:

What impact does your reflection and belief of who Jesus is have on others? _____

_____

_____

_____

_____

SECTION TWO

HOW WE ARE MENTORED

Chapter 5

SCRIPTURE MENTORS US

IF YOU'VE EVER purchased something from the Swedish brand IKEA, you know that assembly is required... and not just three or four parts, but the entire item—down to the nuts and bolts! You would never be able to assemble your dresser or couch without the instruction manual. When it comes to mentorship (being advised, trained, and guided), we are desperate for direction in a similar way. However, because we have a relationship with God, we *always* have access to an instruction manual.

In Section One, we built a foundation for what we believe, who we are, and who Jesus is. These core beliefs and identity work are crucial for knowing how we are to be mentored, as we will choose mentors in alignment with this foundation. The first place we should be looking for mentorship is in the Bible. Who better to mentor us than our Creator, the One who made us in His image?

The Bible was penned by men but inspired by the Holy Spirit, and it is the most important source of truth we have. In a world where people are quick to craft ideologies that aren't in line with the ways of God, we must know Scripture. In fact, the Bible says that the Word IS God.

"In the beginning was the Word, and the Word was with God, and the Word was God." (John 1:1)

Sadly, the Bible often sits as a dust collector on the shelves of most homes. We are quick to read the latest best-selling novel or self-help book, and many believers spend more time in daily devotional books than they do in the Word. While devotionals can be great inspirational reads, we must not let them replace the Bible. We must connect with God in the Word and get to know the truth—the best place to start in our journey through mentorship in every area of our lives.

WHERE DO I START?

If you are somewhat new to the Bible, it's important to understand it's not necessarily a book you read straight through from cover to cover, although you can! There are many Bible studies that take you through the entire Bible in one year that I encourage everyone to do. I've done it twice and it's fascinating what you learn or pick up from reading the same thing.

My husband, Thomas, was raised in Sweden. Although a more secular country, the church is actually run by the Government. In his late 20s, Thomas traveled to the U.S. for his network marketing business. While at a conference, he heard the late Zig Ziglar on stage for the first time. Thomas was fascinated by the gentle spirit and love that radiated from him.

He was able to visit Ziglar backstage to have a personal conversation about success and leadership principles. Thomas asked him, "Mr. Ziglar, what is it that radiates from you?"

Zig answered, "Son, read your Bible."

Since Thomas had never really read the Bible, he purchased one and read it cover to cover. When he got to the New Testament and learned the story of Jesus and the offer of salvation, Thomas accepted Christ as his Savior. While this is an unusual story and way to be converted, it shows that just picking up the Bible can change your life.

If you're looking for a place to start, I direct people to the book of John. To me, the book of John is like the CliffsNotes of truth. Starting from the beginning, which we talked about in the first section of this chapter, the story of Jesus' birth, life, death, and resurrection is woven throughout the entire book in beautiful, poetic language. The book of John is part of the Gospels—Matthew, Mark, Luke, and John—with each of their writers documenting the life of Jesus from their perspective. You will find fascinating connections throughout these four books, as many stories intersect. For instance, the story of Jesus walking on the water is found in Matthew 14:22-34, Mark 6:45-53, and John 6:5-21.

For direction and teaching, Paul wrote 14 letters to the churches of that time to instruct them in their Christian faith. One of my favorite letters of Paul's is to the Ephesians, as it's a beautiful overview of the privilege and responsibility of our faith in peaceful, meditative writing. Take the time to explore these letters to grow in your faith and knowledge of the way of Jesus and what it looks like to follow Him.

As we explored earlier, the Old Testament is filled with prophecies about the coming Messiah in books like Isaiah, Ezekiel, Jeremiah, and Daniel.

You can also find comfort and wisdom in the Old Testament by reading through Psalms and Proverbs. In fact, Proverbs has 31 chapters and can easily be read over the course of a month, one chapter per day. Proverbs gives us God's wisdom in all relations of life. In the heart of the Bible, right in the middle, we find intimate expressions of praise, lament, and hymns in the book of Psalms.

The first book of the Bible, Genesis, describes how the world was formed in the story of creation. A fascinating study that confirms the creation story with facts and evidence was conducted by Pastor Ken Ham, CEO of the Creation Museum, and can be found online at www.answersingenesis.org. A Biblical apologist (a defender and debater of Christian theology), Pastor Ken is best known for his 2014 debate with Evolutionist Bill Nye. I highly recommend studying and learning from his books and teachings to strengthen your belief in God and creation. Learning the truth about creation is critical because this is the stake in the ground that contradicts what many of us were taught in school.

The last book of the Bible, Revelation, is one of the most avoided and misunderstood books. It's important to read Revelation because it gives a powerful perspective on the fact that faithfulness to God, though costly now, brings an eternal reward beyond compare. I have found courage reading Revelation because when the enemy attacks, we are reminded that Satan is already defeated. We can have confidence that we have a sovereign God ruling over all of history, even when things are hard and we feel that we are losing ground.

The more familiar we are with God's Word, the better we will be equipped in life—it's like having a personal mentor available at our fingertips at all times! Through the Bible, we find practical wisdom, encouragement, character building, guidelines, and most of all, an encounter with God who created us. The Bible also shows us God's character—holy, unchanging, faithful, gracious, and loving, just to name a few. Without knowing what the Word says about God, how will we be able to stay anchored as we move forward in our purpose?

Here are a few tips for reading the Bible:

1. **Find a Bible that works for you.** There are all kinds of Bibles available: large print, wide margins, soft or hardcover, different translations, and even study Bibles with commentary built in! Head to a Christian bookstore and take a look around—find something you can see yourself reading every day. I prefer a mid-size, soft leather, so it's easy to carry with me from room to room and when I travel. I also like the large print and versions with red font denoting Jesus' words.

2. **Set a time every day to spend in the Word.** Make it your priority. In fact, make it a non-negotiable. Before I go to bed, I check to see my obligations and intentionally set the alarm to schedule the most important appointment of my day—my quiet time with the Lord. I like to use a highlighter pen and small Post-It tabs when I read. Since the Bible is our *personal* owner's manual, feel free to mark it

up! Write notes, dates, prayers—whatever helps you digest what you're reading.

3. **Ask God where to direct you in Scripture.** You might be surprised if you simply ask God to direct you to what Scripture He wants to speak to you through! The more you commune with Him, the easier this becomes. I encourage you to just ask: "Lord, what book (or chapter) of the Bible do you want me to read today?"

4. **Take your Bible with you wherever you go.** Even from room to room! I keep mine by my computer when I do video appointments, as I will often use it as a reference. You can even bring it with you in your bag or purse as you go about your day, and if you find yourself waiting or on a lunch break, you can read and connect with God instead of scrolling on your phone.

WRONG WAY, JONAH!

There are many characters in the Bible whom can learn practical and life-changing lessons from. My oldest grandchild is named Jonah, and now that he's a teenager, he smiles and rolls his eyes when I start talking about the character Jonah. In the short book of Jonah in the Old Testament, we learn that God speaks to Jonah and tells him to go to the great city of Nineveh and preach against it because of its wickedness. Frightened to obey, Jonah ran away from the Lord and jumped on a ship bound for Tarshish. Can you imagine? "Wow, OK, I escaped that calling. Whew!"

Well, those who are familiar with the book of Jonah know how that story ended. The Lord sent a great storm, and Jonah was thrown overboard only to land in the belly of a whale for three days and three nights. Not only did everyone on the boat vow to follow the Lord, but Jonah also prayed while inside the whale, vowing to make good on his calling, saying, "Salvation comes from the Lord." Then the Lord commanded the whale to release Jonah to dry land.

This time Jonah obeyed the word of the Lord and went to Nineveh. The king and the people of Nineveh believed Jonah and turned from their evil ways. When God saw this, he relented and did not bring on them the destruction he had threatened.

What's the lesson here? Obey God.

My son Nathaniel has four daughters, and recently his family was in town for a soccer tournament for the two oldest, AmmaLee and Ophelia. While on the sidelines with the family, Ophelia's team was on the field. One of the players, somewhat new to the game, began to charge in the wrong direction. Without thinking, I yelled out, "Wrong way, Jonah!"

My daughter Nicole (Jonah's mother) was sitting next to me and said, "Mom, Jonah's not playing!"

We all laughed because this is a phrase I say when I see myself or someone going in the wrong direction.

We can learn practical lessons from many characters in the Bible, not just Jonah. Through their stories, we can discover more about the person, their life, and key principles to learn from their mistakes, trials, and triumphs. We can also see their role in God's plan and how these lessons apply to our own lives. Bible characters are human, just like you and me. They are sinners with flaws. Studying them can show us the struggles they faced and how they dealt with them. Entire books are written about lessons from characters in the Bible, so I encourage you to learn more.

Here are a few we can glean from:

The Prodigal Son: The story of the prodigal Son is one of the most insightful, memorable stories that Jesus told while He was on Earth. Through it, Christ brought to light the ravages of sin, the value of true repentance, and the love of the heavenly Father.

Job: Through the life and story of Job, God gives us insight into tremendous pain and suffering, how not to handle someone's grief, and teaches us that even when we suffer the unimaginable, we can choose to hope in God.

Noah: God told Noah to build an ark before it ever rained. Through this story, we learn how to follow God's instruction, even when it seems crazy and the world is laughing.

Mary, Jesus' Mother: An angel came to Mary to tell her that she was pregnant with the Messiah before she was ever married. Through her bravery, we learn to be obedient to God even in fear of what other people think or how our life will be changed.

Abraham: Long before it ever came to pass, God promised this elderly man and his wife, Sarah, a child, and that their ancestry would outnumber the stars in the sky. The story of Abraham teaches us to leave our comfort zone and be patient while waiting on a promise.

Joseph: Joseph was sold into slavery by his own family, whom he later was able to help tremendously because of his royal position. Often referred to as *the coat of many colors*, the story of Joseph teaches us to endure and trust God despite our circumstances and have a vision that sustains us through difficult times.

Mary Magdalene: Jesus Christ cast out seven demons from Mary Magdalene. Because of her great gratitude, she became one of the most faithful followers of Jesus. She sets an example of hope no matter who you are and displays loyalty and love.

David: David was the least likely son to be chosen to reign as king; however, God anointed him before he ever knew it was a possibility. It's not just a story about a kid with a rock and a sling who defeated Goliath. Through David, we learn that God sees, anoints us, and fulfills the call on our life… and how to defeat the giants!

Paul: Paul became a disciple *after* Jesus died! He was a tax collector that persecuted Christians. After his conversion on the road to Damascus, he goes on to preach the gospel, get put in prison, and write over half of the New Testament, teaching us that God uses the most unlikely!

Deborah: God has never been sexist; He has used men and women from the beginning. Deborah was a prophetess, a warrior, a songwriter, and the only female judge to shepherd God's people and lead Israel into battle against their enemies. We learn from her leadership, wisdom, and courage.

Peter: Peter was one of the disciples (also noted as their leader). In fact, in Matthew 16:18, it says, "And I also say to you that you are Peter, and upon this rock I will build My church; and the gates of Hades will not overpower it."

Wow, what an honor! Yet we also read from the gospels that Jesus told Peter that he would deny Jesus three times. Matthew 26:34 says, "Jesus said to him, 'Truly I say to you that this very night, before a rooster crows, you will deny Me three times.'"

Shortly after Jesus was arrested, sure enough, just as Jesus said, Peter denied him three times, and then he heard the rooster crow. How would you feel? Would you leave your faith in shame? Thankfully, it didn't end there. After Jesus rose from the dead, he gave Peter another chance and restored him. We can learn from Peter that nothing can separate us from God's love.

Esther: One of the most popular women in the Bible—with an entire book dedicated to her story—Queen Esther teaches us to have the right attitude to open doors. The saying "for such a time as this" comes from Esther 4:14. In this book, we learn about her beauty and how she became the queen without the king knowing she was a Jew. When her uncle Mordecai learned the fate of the Jewish people through a scheming plan of one of the king's leaders, Haman, Esther had to risk her life by stepping into the forbidden area of the king to plea for the life of her people. She was successful, and Haman was hung on the gallows he prepared for Mordecai. We learn from Esther to be courageous for what we believe in—who knows if you were created for such a time as this!

John the Baptist: John the Baptist was the forerunner, baptizing and preparing people for the coming Messiah, Jesus. He always pointed to the one and only Savior, Jesus. John testified about Jesus in John 1:29-31: "The next day he saw Jesus coming to him, and said, 'Behold, the Lamb of God who takes away the sin of the world! This is He in behalf of whom I said, "After me is coming a Man who has proved to be my superior, because He existed before me." And I did not recognize Him, but so that He would be revealed to Israel, I came baptizing in water.'"

While John baptized with water, Jesus baptized with the Spirit. John spoke the truth, and never apologized or shrunk. He was bold and courageous and never wavered. As a result, we learn that John was beheaded, and his head presented on a platter in Mark 6. We learn from John the Baptist to be humble, courageous and steadfast, and to know your purpose here.

* * *

There are hundreds of characters from the Bible that we can learn from, and these are just a few. I can't encourage you enough to start digging into these stories and intentionally gleaning from their experiences. All Scripture points us to Jesus, and all Scripture is God-breathed and available to teach (and mentor) us!

EMBRACING BIBLICAL PRINCIPLES

The Bible is our ultimate guidebook—the greatest instruction manual ever crafted! As we can see just by looking at these stories, there are endless opportunities to learn, grow, and be led by Scripture. The following are a few key Biblical principles to help you see how you can be actively mentored by the Word as you follow Jesus on the path He set out for you to walk.

SEEK GOD'S DESIRE FOR YOUR LIFE

As we think about the future, whether it involves a career, family, location, or something completely different, it is easy to be tempted to follow our own path—often, the one of least resistance. Though going your own way might look to be easier, I can assure you that it will not be as fruitful as following the way of Jesus!

So, how do we know the way of Jesus?

Well, first, we must get to know Him through Scripture and learn about how we ought to live as His followers.

Our human nature is to fulfill our own desires, but that is not the way of the Christian. The Bible says we must die to ourselves and put off our old selves to follow Jesus! "…put off your old self, which belongs to your former manner of life and is corrupt through deceitful desires, and to be renewed in the spirit of your minds, and to put on the new self, created after the likeness of God in true righteousness and holiness." (Ephesians 4:22-24 ESV)

As I mentioned in Chapter 2, I have found over and over that when I've gotten off track and followed my own wishes without God's confirmation and blessing, the results were not always what I thought they would be. Remember: "Wrong way, Jonah!"

Thankfully, the Holy Spirit helps us identify when we've taken wrong steps, learn from our mistakes, and leads us into wisdom to follow God's path and plan for our lives. When listening and leaning into God's wisdom, we discover the rich reward He has for us.

God is not a vending machine. Instead of praying to bless *our* plans, ask God to reveal *His* plan for your life. Take the time to pray and really know God's will before moving forward. I know I get bullheaded and often want to blaze forward with something I want to do. I've learned to pause, pray, and listen for that still small voice to know what's the right thing to do.

AVOID THE TRAPPINGS OF THIS WORLD

When I say "trappings of the world," I mean that there are false gods all around us. In 2 Corinthians 4:4, we learn that "… the god of this world has blinded the minds of the unbelieving so that they will not see the light of the gospel of the glory of Christ, who is the image of God."

Staying in the Word will help us discern what is in line with God's character and what isn't, which helps us avoid these deceptive trappings that often disguise themselves cleverly to confuse and trick us. We must be able to distinguish between what God says and Satan's distortions of the truth, as it is a crucial part of being mentored and mentoring others.

SEEK GROWTH IN OUR CHARACTER

The Bible also establishes basic tenets of Christian character and behavior. These include the Lordship of Christ over all aspects of our lives and thoughts; the responsibility to love God with our whole being and to love our neighbor as ourselves; the responsibility to pursue righteousness and practice justice and mercy to everyone, and participation in worship and thanksgiving with fellow believers. When we consistently work on developing our character by seeking to be mentored by the Word in how we should live, we will see the fruit in our relationships with other people and be able to practically apply and walk out mentoring others.

NOW IT'S TIME TO DO IT!

When we are intentionally being mentored by Scripture, we will naturally live a life like Jesus. While we will never achieve perfection because Jesus was the only perfect one, we can still strive to become more like Him every day. In doing so, we will effortlessly love and encourage those around us, live a life of gratitude and thanksgiving, and share what we have.

When we make it a habit to be in the Word daily, it becomes a natural part of our life, just like brushing our teeth.

Recently, I was working out in the gym with my trainer and friend Lori, and our conversation drifted to this chapter of the book. She shared with me that while she has a Bible, she puts off picking it up and reading it because she wrote a story in her head that it is confusing and overwhelming. I told her how grateful I was that she shared and that I know so many people feel the same way. I encouraged her to start a new habit that very next morning: dust off the Bible and start reading! I told her that one of my favorite chapters of the Bible is Ephesians, and to start there. Once she began to make it a habit, I encouraged her to read a chapter of Proverbs a day.

Maybe you're just like Lori, telling yourself that it will be too overwhelming to even start. Today is a great day to write a new story and pick it up. Just like working out in the gym, picking up the Bible and making it a daily practice is a matter of discipline. Soon enough, you'll notice a huge difference when you don't.

Water Walker Reflections:

Currently, do you have a daily habit of reading the Bible? If so, what does it look like? If not, what are you waiting for?

_____

_____

_____

_____

_____

_____

Moving forward, what commitment will you make for getting into the Word? _____

_____

_____

_____

_____

How will you hold yourself accountable? (Examples: Joining a Bible study, logging into an app on your phone with reminders, or grabbing a Bible buddy to read with.) _____

_____

_____

_____

_____

Who sets an example in your life of someone that is consistently reading and learning from Scripture? _____

_____

_____

_____

_____

Reach out to that person to ask what their favorite lessons from the Bible are!

What is your "wrong way, Jonah" story, and what lesson did God teach you from that story? _____
_____
_____
_____

What character from the Bible do you most relate to and why? _____
_____
_____
_____

Ripple Effect:

How will those around you be positively impacted with your renewed commitment to being mentored by Scripture? ___
_____
_____
_____

Chapter 6

BEING MENTORED BY THE HOLY SPIRIT

IT WAS 7:15 a.m. on Tuesday, November 10, 2020—the final day of my three-day fast and prayer with my Esther Circle of friends; this was the day that changed the trajectory of my life. I woke to a light rain, closed my eyes, and sang this beautiful song in my mind:

> "Rain, rain on me, open the windows of Heaven. Open up the heavens, pouring out a blessing, Lord, we need refreshing till it overflows. Oh I hear the sound of revival rain. I hear the sound; I hear the sound."
>
> —"Rain," Leeland

The soft rain outside blended with the soothing sound of the song in my head and put me back to sleep. Suddenly, I was brought into a beautiful dream. I was lifted above the atmosphere and sensed I was hovering over what appeared to be Texas, United States. To the north, I saw Canada, and to the east and west, I saw America from ocean to ocean. Just as I was getting my bearings as to where I was in the dream, the most incredible experience unfolded before my eyes. I watched in awe as the clouds of the atmosphere rolled from one side to the other. The picture in my mind was similar to the parting of the Red Sea like in the story of Moses, but it wasn't water, it was clouds. The parting created an opening over the Mississippi River that runs north to south across the United States.

I couldn't believe what I saw next: Mighty angels were holding the clouds in place at the parting of the atmosphere. I suddenly looked above and there were babies, young children, and people of all ages celebrating, dancing, and laughing in unison. More than the vision was the *feeling*. Imagine your favorite sports team winning the biggest game of the season and the celebration that ensues. Now multiply that sheer excitement by 100. That's how it felt! I was completely caught up in the exhilaration when I looked down below the atmosphere to see what they were celebrating.

The only way I can describe the next several minutes of my vision was to relate it to the *life flashing before your eyes* sort of experience. I've heard of this happening to people, and it always fascinated me. I saw secrets of the world that I sensed had been hidden for a very long time being revealed and playing like a movie in fast-forward. As I watched, these words were spoken to me:

"For there is nothing hidden that will not be disclosed, and nothing concealed that will not be known or brought out into the open."

I knew this to be from Scripture, found in Luke 8:17: "For nothing is concealed that will not become evident, nor anything hidden that will not be known and come to light."

Then I realized what the celebration above was about: things that were hidden in darkness were finally coming to light. At the same time, behind my right shoulder were people watching in disbelief from a distance. This group of people was on the same "level" (for lack of better word) as me. Those celebrating were above the atmosphere, while these people to my side and I were on the same level as the parting of the atmosphere. Intriguingly, they had a shadow cast on them. I have no idea where these words came from, but in my mind, I kept hearing "gray goo." It was so odd. There were different shades of the goo; some was dark or black, while others were lighter.

With everything going on at once—the celebration above, the angels holding the cloud wave, the revelation below, and those with gray goo observing—you would think it would be difficult to focus, but for some reason, I was able to experience and feel all four perspectives happening at the same time.

Just like me, those with the gray goo were watching the revelation unfold below the atmosphere. Their eyes were fixed there, so it became clear to me that they couldn't see the celebration above as I could.

The next part of my vision was astonishing because not only was I able to observe what they were doing, but I could also sense what they were *feeling*. As they watched the truth unfold and become evident, the gray goo came off some of them. Some, but not all. I observed those with lighter shades of goo quickly transform, but others, those with the darker goo, did not. I want to make it clear this was nothing about skin color; it was a cloak like an aura or shadow.

Those that released this shadowy goo quickly moved through the parted atmosphere toward those celebrating. Since I was able to also feel what they were feeling, I sensed tremendous shame, sorrow, and shock.

As this was happening, these words came to me over and over: "Do not have a haughty heart, have a humble heart."

As they greeted those celebrating, those passing through the atmosphere were expecting to be shamed and ridiculed. They were shocked to sense the most beautiful love, reconciliation, and forgiveness.

After those that released the goo passed through the wave opening, those behind me with darker goo plunged below into the opening where we all watched. Suddenly, the angels released the waves, covering the fallen and the movie-like scene unfolding. As this was happening, there were visions rising above the waves from beneath. It's difficult to describe what emerged from below because it was more a knowledge given to me, instead of a picture. I saw a celebration that wealth was intended for God's good, and the suppressed knowledge of natural healing medicine, energy, and technology was being released.

As I watched the celebration, to my left (west) above the atmosphere, I saw God sitting at a table in all His glory. Words cannot describe the love and power radiating from His majestic presence. He waved for me to come by Him. I was frozen.

Me?

It was clear. *Yes, me.*

As I walked toward Him, I fell to my knees and praised Him, but also dropped my head in shame. "I am not worthy," I said. However, He picked me up and told me that He loved me. I knew that He had given me this vision to give me the confidence to trust Him and show me that He put me where I am for a purpose.

I woke up shortly after and lay in awe for a few moments. Then, I quickly grabbed paper and a pen to journal about my vision so I wouldn't forget any of the key details. I prayed and asked, "God, what do I do with this?" The Holy Spirit immediately said, "When Thomas [my husband] wakes, tell him first. Then tell your brothers and your circle of friends." I then sensed he would lead me with more instruction thereafter. The beautiful thing about our relationship with our Heavenly Father is that it is ongoing. He walks with us and talks with us, and He uses Holy Spirit to guide us.

This dream was a source of mentorship for me, and God used it to confirm my purpose and direction for my life. God not only mentors us with His word, but He gifts us with a helper, the Holy Spirit!

John 14:16-17 says, "I will ask the Father, and He will give you another Helper, so that He may be with you forever; the Helper is the Spirit of truth, whom the world cannot receive, because it does not see Him or know Him; but you know Him because He remains with you and will be in you."

And there's more...

"If we live by the Spirit, let's follow the Spirit as well." (Galatians 5:25)

Found right in Scripture, there it is! One of the greatest mentorship sources is the Holy Spirit. My dream didn't mentor me; the Holy Spirit did!

HOW DOES HOLY SPIRIT MENTOR US?

In Joel Chapter 2, we see that there are many different ways God communicates through the Holy Spirit:

"It will come about after this That I will pour out My Spirit on all mankind; And your sons and your daughters will prophesy, Your old men will have dreams, Your young men will see visions. And even on the male and female servants I will pour out My Spirit in those days." (Joel 2:28-29)

While these are not the only ways the Holy Spirit speaks to us, and thus mentors us, they are a great start. Let's explore a few of these in more detail.

DREAMS

One of the ways God speaks to us through the Spirit is through dreams. Now, of course, not every dream is from the Lord, and we must be careful to check them against the Word. One of the easiest ways to confirm that a dream is from God is when it can be confirmed with Scripture.

The dream I mentioned at the beginning of this chapter was especially life-changing for me because it spoke to me in such a way that I clearly understood the mission God had given me. For accountability, I shared my dream with my inner circle—my husband, brothers, and friends. They prayed with me for discernment and confirmation. We were fascinated to see so many pieces of the dream in Scripture. For instance, I don't usually use the word "haughty" that was clearly spoken to me in my dream. My friend Karen pointed out that it's the first sin of the six sins God hates the most.

Proverbs 6:16-19 says: "There are six things that the Lord hates, Seven that are an abomination to Him: Haughty eyes, a lying tongue, And hands that shed innocent blood, A heart that devises wicked plans, Feet that run rapidly to evil, A false witness who declares lies, And one who spreads strife among brothers."

A dream from the Holy Spirit will often strengthen your faith and focus on your path of God's will for your life. Here are some immediate changes I made starting that day:

- I became thirstier for His Word.
- I spent more time walking and talking with Him throughout my day.
- I became more confident, courageous, and bold in my communication.
- I readjusted my inner circle.
- I became clear in my priorities, saying "no" to things I used to say "yes" to.
- I started a Bible study.
- I started speaking at faith-based conferences.
- I wrote this book.

In addition, I've had other dreams right before waking, which have given me guidance for a variety of things:

- An idea for a work project
- A solution for family or friendship issues that needed attention

- Before my first Bible Study, the Holy Spirit gave me clarity with the phrases "think eternity" and "fishers of men."

While in the planning stages of this book, the publishers and I were searching for the finishing touches of the story arc and chapters. Again, right before waking, the Holy Spirit gave me not only the name of the first four chapters, but the *why* behind them and the message. When Holy Spirit is involved, you will likely sense peace in your heart—a confirmation or a *knowing*.

SCRIPTURE

In Chapter 5, we discussed some of the ways Scripture mentors us. Sometimes, the Holy Spirit will literally drop a Scripture verse in your mind. This can be startling when it happens, but when it does, jot it down quickly and go to your Bible. (This is another good reason to keep your Bible with you at all times!) Often, the Holy Spirit illuminates the Word and shows you exactly what you need to see and when you need to see it.

My dear friends Kristin and Daryl VanderVeen live on two and a half acres in the heart of the fruit and nut farmland area of central California. They envisioned turning their beautiful backyard into a wedding venue. Kristin works from home as an entrepreneur in the same company as me, while Daryl is a self-employed electrical contractor. In May 2020, churches were closing with COVID lockdowns. Daryl heard a message from Pastor Jack Hibbs encouraging pastors not to close their churches. (Hibbs, the Pastor of Calvary Chapel in Chino Hills,

California, never closed his church.) Daryl enthusiastically passed it on to his own pastor and other friends, only to have his message fall on deaf ears.

Frustrated, one day, Daryl stood outside in their flower garden and prayed to God, "You've got to do something, this just isn't right!" Easter came and went, and churches were still shut down. Daryl suddenly felt a quickening in his spirit, and he knew that God had given them that place for a reason. He was flooded with Scripture affirmations and confirmation to move forward with hosting church in their backyard. The first Scripture God revealed to him was from Proverbs 27:10, saying, "Do not boast about tomorrow, For you do not know what a day may bring."

This reminded Him how we make plans, but God will often disrupt our plans with HIS plans. Daryl became very aware of that when this Scripture was laid on his heart. The second Scripture was from Proverbs 16:9: "The mind of a person plans his way, But the LORD directs his steps." Again, just a confirmation to listen for God's plan, not ours.

Sometime later, Daryl was making plans to reach out to pastors to set up a schedule when he clearly heard God say, "No, Daryl, I want *you* to do it."

"What?" Daryl immediately argued with God, "I'm an electrician!" Then he heard the most profound whisper from God, "Daryl, what if this is the way it's supposed to be?"

Just like what happened with my book, the Holy Spirit downloaded the first two weeks' worth of Sunday sermons to Daryl. He jokingly says, "Well, as an electrician, I'm working with something extremely powerful that you can't see, so it is being obedient to God's calling." God was calling this electrician to plug into God's powerful plan. They've been hosting what they call "Country Church" every Sunday ever since.

RED LIGHTS / GREEN LIGHTS / YELLOW LIGHTS

Sometimes you will receive a *check-in-your-spirit* type of feeling to not move forward with something. Some people call it a gut feeling. This can be the Holy Spirit giving you a *red light* to stop what you are doing and re-assess. This recently happened to me before a trip to Sweden in December 2021. I was packed and ready to go when I felt a check in my spirit. I prayed to God to give me three signs by 8 a.m., as I would need to make a decision and let Thomas know whether or not I was actually going on this trip. Sure enough, three signs appeared, and I knew I was not supposed to travel. Thomas understood and gave me his blessing to stay behind.

When I returned from dropping Thomas at the airport and walked into the door of our home, I prayed, "OK, God. This is the law of the vacuum. Show me your will for me these ten days alone." That is when God dropped this book in my heart. While some red lights are to avoid dangers, this was a red-light moment to reveal God's plan for this book to me.

Then there are times when you feel drawn, prompted, or led to something. These leadings are your *green lights* from the Holy Spirit.

The energizing feeling you get from these green lights is so exhilarating! It actually feels like God has His big hand on the small of your back, literally pushing you forward. It's like the lyrics from the song "Break My Stride" by Matthew Wilder: "Aint nothing gonna break my stride; nobody's gonna slow me down, on no, I got to keep on moving!"

Cheryl, one of the members of my Bible Study, shared during one series that God had put it on her heart to write a children's book based on characters in the Bible. She was all smiles when she shared her excitement; it felt as if God had His hand on her, pushing her through the door of an adventure! A definite green light.

Sometimes, you'll feel as if you are in a holding pattern. As you seek guidance and direction, all you can sense is a feeling of uncertainty. These are your *yellow light* moments to yield and wait. Being a get-things-done kind of person, moments like these drive me crazy, and it happened to me while writing this book! I did not know if I should share my November 2020 dream. I told my publisher and editing team about the dream, but that I was in prayer if I should even include it in this book. I simply gave the request to the Lord in prayer and asked Him to reveal the answer in His time. Then I let it go and trusted Him.

I'm learning not to move without that *green light* confirmation, and it's been a tough lesson for me, but I am getting better with practice and time. After a few weeks, in my early morning prayer time, God gave me His plan of where to put the dream. It fit like the perfect puzzle piece.

Learn to recognize your "wrong way, Jonah" *red lights*, your "nothing's gonna stop me" *green lights*, and your "wait upon the Lord" *yellow lights*.

WORD OF KNOWLEDGE

There are also times when you will receive a word of knowledge. This recently happened to me when I was following a dear friend and leader in my business from the UK. She had two daughters, and, unfortunately, had a traumatic birth with her second. After that experience, she and her husband vowed to not have any more children. Ten years later, they decided to move forward and have a third baby. Social media has a way of bringing us into people's experiences and emotions, as Daniella beautifully shared her journey. In August 2022, the weekend before her scheduled C-section the following Tuesday, I sensed the stress and fear she was feeling. So, I reached out to her to pray for her and the baby.

Then, the Sunday night before the birth, she posted a gift she would give whoever correctly predicted the birth weight of her baby. I simply closed my eyes and said, "Heavenly Father, what is the weight of Dani's baby?"

Immediately, I heard 5 pounds 8 ounces. So, I commented to my friend, "Dani, your beautiful, healthy baby is 5 pounds 8 ounces. God Bless your growing family."

Sure enough, the baby was exactly 5 pounds 8 ounces, but I asked Dani to give the gift to someone in need. It's amazing how God works if you only ask. He will show you!

PROPHECY

Prophecy is one of the nine gifts of the Holy Spirit mentioned in 1 Corinthians 12. It's simply when the Holy Spirit gives you a specific word or message to convey to someone else—to hear what God is saying about them and tell them. Different from the Old Testament *role* of a prophet, what we're talking about here is the *gift* of prophecy. I do not believe there is anything greater than to be able to receive a direct, clear prophetic word from the Lord to be able to give to someone else in order to help edify and build them up.

This happened to me when I received a prophetic word from my friend Sue. She called me out of the blue a little over a year ago, saying she had a dream about me being pregnant. Now, at my age, that is no longer possible, and she knows this! When she asked God to interpret the dream, He gave her the interpretation and instructed her to give me a word. She shared that God was birthing something new in my life, something *big*. We prayed over this prophecy and asked the Holy Spirit to reveal His message. This happened shortly before my dream that led to this book!

On another occasion, I was boarding a flight bound for Las Vegas, where I was speaking in front of several thousand people in the Grand Garden Arena. I was reviewing my notes for my stage presentation and started feeling panicky. I went to turn my phone off and saw a post with a picture of two blue angels in the night sky. Reading further, someone commented that a blue stone (lapis lazuli or sapphire) is mentioned to be found in God's throne room.

Ezekiel 1:26 says, "Now above the expanse that was over their heads there was something resembling a throne, like lapis lazuli in appearance; and on that which resembled a throne, high up, was a figure with the appearance of a man."

The theory is that when the angels are in God's throne room getting direction, they often appear blue when they come to carry out their instructions. I laid back in my chair and contemplated this beautiful thought. At that moment, I heard the Holy Spirit say to me, "Do not be afraid. My blue angels will be with you when you speak."

I was grateful I shared this with my husband while we were waiting to check into our hotel because the next morning, I received a text from my friend Sharon. It was simply a picture of the Navy's Blue Angel jets. After the picture came, an audio text delivered, saying, "Donna, you probably think this is crazy, but I was praying over your message you'll be speaking in Vegas, and God told me to tell you that His blue angels will be with you. I argued with Him, 'What? What does that mean? Donna is going to think I'm crazy!'"

She Googled "blue angels" and found the Navy jets. Being obedient, she told me, "God told me to tell you His blue angels will be with you." I showed Thomas her picture and text, and all he could say was, "Wow." What a beautiful confirmation the Holy Spirit gave Sharon to comfort and encourage me. She was right; I had no fear backstage and felt the Holy Spirit and those blue angels with me as I spoke.

Previously, anytime I was waiting backstage, I would be so anxious that I'd hyperventilate. That day, I simply prayed a decree and declaration:

"God, I know I normally can't breathe before I go on stage, but that is really stressful. I will now go on stage confident and breathing with ease because I know You are with me." Immediately, I was calm and at peace. This is now my new normal. I will only speak of being nervous in the past tense.

These are just a few ways the Holy Spirit speaks to (and therefore mentors) us, and I encourage you to lean in and ask

Him to show you the ways He may already be speaking to you. Don't be surprised if you start to hear Him more!

Taking this a step further, Holy Spirit is not only your best mentor, but He's the best guide to mentor *others*.

DISCOVER YOUR GIFTS

The gifts of the Spirit are alive and well today and readily available to us as followers of Christ. However, you'll need to lean in and discover your unique gift (or gifts). Now, spiritual gifts are different from talents. Natural talents are often something you're born with and can develop and practice. Only spiritual gifts are given when you are born again. Gifts of the Spirit are also different from the *fruits* of the Spirit, which we will naturally exude when we abide with Him. The fruits of the Spirit are found in Galatians 5:22-23, and they are love, joy, peace, patience, kindness, generosity, faithfulness, gentleness, and self-control.

It is right to earnestly desire and *ask* for your spiritual gifts! In 1 Corinthians 14:1, Paul tells us that our longing, pursuit, and coveting of the gifts of the Spirit is a Holy desire!

So, what are the gifts of the Holy Spirit?

In 1 Corinthians 12:4-6, we read, "Now there are varieties of gifts, but the same Spirit. And there are varieties of ministries, and the same Lord. There are varieties of effects, but the same God who works all things in all *persons*." Then Paul goes on to list and describe the gifts:

- Wisdom
- Knowledge

- Faith
- Healing
- Miracles
- Prophecy
- Discerning of Spirits
- Different Kinds of Tongues
- Interpretation of Tongues

When you discover and activate your spiritual gifts, you are owning your part of the body of Christ and living in harmony with those around you who have other gifts and strengths. It's a beautiful thing when we all use our gifts and witness others using theirs!

But how do we activate the gifts? Well, it's like turning on a light. Just flipping the switch won't work if there's no lightbulb. Discovering is *receiving* your gifts, and activating is *using* your gifts. Neglecting to act is like a construction worker who fills up his toolbelt but sits on the couch. The Holy Spirit's gifts are the tools for the job at hand!

Jesus explains this with the parable of the talents in Matthew 25:14-30, wherein Jesus tells a story of a master who went away on a journey, but before he did, he gave talents to his servants. One servant got four talents, another two, and another only one. He did this according to the ability demonstrated by the servants.

When the master returned, he inquired of the servants about what they did with the money that he gave them. Two servants multiplied what they received by using the money to make more, while one servant buried the talent that was given to him and was punished because of it. We should learn from this parable and increase what we have been given by being good stewards. A good steward acts with the gifts God gives so that others may benefit.

Paul also teaches us in 1 Corinthians 12:1-2, "Now concerning spiritual gifts, brothers and sisters, I do not want you to be unaware. You know that when you were pagans, you were led astray to the mute idols, however you were led."

This is complex and often misunderstood, but I want you to be informed and knowledgeable. Remember how you were when you didn't know God? Led from one phony god to another, never knowing what you were doing, just doing it because everybody else did it? It's different in this life. God wants us to use our intelligence, to seek and to understand as well as we can.

You may or may not already be aware of what *your* spiritual gifts are after being born again. Would you like to take a Spiritual gifts test to help you start to discover what they might? Go to:

www.biblesprout.com/articles/god/holy-spirit/spiritual -gifts-test/

My test results are leadership, faith, and evangelism. While I knew these were my gifts prior to the test, it was interesting to have it confirmed.

As you go about your journey of discovering and activating your unique giftings, it is important not to compare yours with the people around you. We are all given different gifts that work together for good. Once you know your gifts, you can be more effective in stewarding your time, talents, and treasures.

C.O.M.E.

Living a supernatural life filled with signs and wonders is a normal part of the Christian lifestyle. As believers, the same power that raised Jesus from the dead is living *inside* of us. Read that again!

Romans 8:11 says, "But if the Spirit of Him who raised Jesus from the dead dwells in you, He who raised Christ Jesus from the dead will also give life to your mortal bodies through His Spirit who dwells in you."

Just think of that; the same supernatural power lives in us as believers! So how do we approach mentorship with this in mind? How can we be mentored by Holy Spirit into living a radical life filled with signs and wonders?

We step out of the boat, we heed the call of Jesus to "come," and we ask the Spirit to fill us.

When Peter and the disciples were in the boat and saw Jesus walking on the water to approach them, Peter simply asked in Mathew 14:28-29, "Lord, if it be thou, bid me come unto thee upon the waters. And he said, Come. And Peter went down from the boat, and walked upon the waters to come to Jesus."

The following is an acronym based on the word "come," and can be used as a practical guide to activating the spiritual gifts you're meant to use and live out.

C: CHOOSE TO ACTIVATE YOUR SPIRITUAL GIFTS

You have a *soul*, you have a *spirit*, and they live in your *body*.

Because of sin, your spirit was dead before receiving Jesus and the Holy Spirit. Now that it's alive, you must *awaken* your spirit! We become a new creature in Christ, so fan the flame and *activate* your gifts! One way I do this is to boldly state aloud: "I decree and declare that, because of Jesus, I have been unified forever with the Holy Spirit, who never leaves me."

O: OBEY & TRUST FULLY IN JESUS

Wholeheartedly surrendering to Jesus and giving Him a blank check in the form of your life can often feel like you are falling off a cliff. That's what "letting go and letting God" feels like. You must trust with your entire being that God has your back; that He will help you and take care of you. How often do you say you've "turned it over to God," only to take it back? Let go of the push and pull. Surrender and trust Jesus fully.

Your trust equals faith, which also equals risk. Miracles don't take place until you put yourself into a position of risk. Speak out and act on what God is revealing to you.

In my own life, it often feels like I'm standing alone. While most people would rather please others and not speak or act when the Holy Spirit moves, I have chosen to stand with God. My priorities are such that God is first, so how the world wants me to behave is really none of my business.

What at first seems like I'm standing alone ends up as not only inspiration to empower others, but also to evangelism and to lead people to the Lord. You just never know whose life you will touch, so who are we to hold back? Fully trust Jesus. You will meet many in Heaven who will come up and thank you for using the gifts of the spirit inside you, and in so doing, saving their lives.

M: MOVE (AND KEEP MOVING)

God's heart is to have us share the *good news* with the world around us. This is something to be excited about, and we have the privilege of telling the rest of the world about the hope of Jesus! However, we can't do anything if we're standing still.

Play full-out on the field of life. I'm a Green Bay Packers fan, and I like to use this analogy: "You don't see Aaron Rogers sitting on the bench (unless he's injured). Don't be a bench-sitter; get in the game!"

E: ENCOURAGE & HELP THOSE AROUND YOU

Activating the Holy Spirit in you will mentor others—the great Helper works through you to help others. We are called to love and serve others as Christ loves and serves us! After all, they will know we follow Christ by our love. Love is a verb; love *does*.

Paul shows us in 1 Corinthians 12:31 that the great filter for all the spiritual gifts is love: "But earnestly desire the greater gifts. And yet, I am going to show you a far better way."

Paul is not saying to choose love *over* your gifts; he is saying to choose love *with* your gifts. Just as Jesus demonstrates his love when dealing with those who yet believe, ask yourself these questions before using your spiritual gifts: Is what I'm about to do *loving* and *kind*? Or is it *self-seeking*, *boastful*, or *dishonoring*?

In my business, I teach people to *attract* others to our brand, not hit them over the head with it. The first strategy encourages people to lean in and want to learn more; the second strategy often causes people to run.

It is important to discover and use our spiritual gifts, but above all else, do it in love. In doing so, you are of the most help to the world. Imagine the imprint and impact (the Ripple Effect) you can make on the world knowing you have the help of your personal mentor, the Holy Spirit.

* * *

The world is full of choices for whom you choose to mentor you. God laid out a beautiful plan for us to be first mentored by His Word and His Spirit. In the next chapter, we'll explore how other people can mentor you as well. As you move along, I would advise you to make these two resources—Scripture and Holy Spirit—the foundation of your mentorship model. All else will add to it.

"Anyone who listens to my teaching and follows it is wise, like a person who builds a house on solid rock. Though the rain comes in torrents and the floodwaters rise and the winds beat against that house, it won't collapse because it is built on bedrock." (Mathew 7:24-25)

Water Walker Reflections:

Have you ever had a dream where you felt God was speaking to you or showing you a specific vision? Journal here: ___

_____

_____

_____

_____

_____

What Scriptures and prayer partners helped you confirm?

_____

_____

_____

_____

_____

Place a Journal, or paper and pen by your nightstand to write down ways the Holy Spirit may be speaking to you through your dreams.

Take the Spiritual Gifts Test. What are your Top 3 Gifts?

1. _____

2. _____

3. _____

What are some ways you've noticed you naturally operate in your gifts? _____

_____

_____

_____

What are some ways you feel the Holy Spirit mentoring you?

_____

_____

_____

_____

Ripple Effect:

Journal some ways you will make an impact on others when you fully embrace your gifts and walk hand in hand with Holy Spirit: _____

_____

_____

_____

_____

Who are fellow believers that can help you discern and test the gifts or dreams you are receiving? _____

_____

_____

_____

_____

Chapter 7

BEING MENTORED BY PEOPLE

WE ARE NOT mentored only by Scripture, Holy Spirit, or people individually; we are mentored by a combination of the three. Seek mentorship as a synergistic and harmonious approach, always using Scripture as the foundation. It's like the strength of a three-strand cord or a rope. The three-stranded cord metaphor is found in Ecclesiastes 4:12: "And if one can overpower him who is alone, two can resist him. A cord of three strands is not quickly torn apart." Though talking about mentorship as a three-stranded cord isn't what this verse is talking about, we can apply similar principles.

The three-stranded mentorship cord is a beautiful check and balance system; when receiving mentorship from others, take it to the Lord in prayer and verify in Scripture. People are human and naturally flawed, but the Word of God is unfailing. If you were only mentored by other people without testing it with prayer and Scripture, you could end up "drinking the Kool-Aid."

If you're not familiar with where this term came from, in 1978, the cult leader Jim Jones, who had an unconventional, deranged message, started a camp of followers in Jonestown, Guyana. When family members received disturbing reports from their loved ones, U.S. Congressman Leo Ryan traveled to Jones's camp to investigate. As he was leaving, he and four people traveling with him were shot to death. Following those murders, Jones commanded his followers to drink cyanide-laced punch, starting with the children. In all, over 900 people died, simply by following the command of this deranged leader.

I wonder if those people had a better understanding of Scripture and a relationship with the Holy Spirit if things would have been different. I'm willing to bet it would!

I encourage you to make it a point to seek out mentorship in a three-stranded approach by making it a habit to read Scripture daily, commune with the Holy Spirit, walk in your gifts, and choose like-minded individuals to pour into you.

As we dive into what it looks like to be mentored by other people, it is important to test what and who is influencing you. Just like that rubber ducky being tossed around in the sea, be careful not to mindlessly follow people without giving it careful thought. You don't want other people creating or guiding the direction of your life. That's a very personal decision. Make that *your* choice, based on the work *you've* done and continue on *your* desired path.

In fact, that's the reason Section One of this book is so important. You must create a firm foundation for your life from which all things flow. When you are clear about who you are (based on who God says you are), you'll make wise choices for whom you allow to mentor you. Because you are beginning to align your life with this foundation, you'll find that your surroundings will change (meaning the people you surround yourself with will change), and the resources around you will naturally give you access to the mentors that are the right fit for you. In Section Three, we will explore being mentored in each area of your life to give you practical, targeted application.

THE IMPORTANCE OF DISCERNMENT

Once I accepted Christ, I couldn't get enough of the Word, so other influences were not attractive to me anymore. Holy Spirit gave me—and will give you—a tool to use; it's called discernment. Discernment is the ability to decide between truth and error, right and wrong. It is the process of making careful distinctions in our thinking about truth. In other words, the ability to think with discernment is synonymous with the ability to think Biblically. It is critical to use this gift of discernment for choosing mentors and other influencers, such as coaches or advisors, in your life.

In addition to personal mentors, influence over you (access to you) comes in many other forms: the conversations you have, books you read, podcasts and music you listen to, and the activities you choose. With the advent of social media, our access to being influenced can feel like a firehose when not self-regulated.

However, you must understand that what you allow in will either fuel or poison you. You must exercise discernment in what you allow access to and absorb. Ephesians 4:14 carries a clear warning to not be "tossed here and there by waves and carried about by every wind of doctrine, by the trickery of people, by craftiness in deceitful scheming." False teachings and deception are part of life, so learning how to discern what is fruitful for your life, whether it is a person, a TV show, or a radio station, is essential for your personal and spiritual growth.

HOW DO I FIND A MENTOR?

A meaningful mentor-mentee relationship is unlike any other personal or work relationship. People often mistake mentorship as a "let's sit down and I'll ask you to mentor me, and we'll have a weekly meeting" type of deal. However, that is not the case. It's so much more! A mentor is a wise and trusted counselor or teacher that imparts a meaningful and inspiring relationship. Mentors serve as a guide to their mentee, and they exchange value that is not monetary. Often, a mentor will inspire the mentee to *pay it forward.* The beautiful part about mentorship is the ripple effect and influence you have to then mentor others.

Now, it's important to note that there's a difference between a mentor and an advisor or coach. Typically, coaches and advisors are for hire to improve performance, meet goals, or resolve challenges; it's a business transaction.

Let's move into some practical ways you can find or discern if a mentor is right for you:

1. PRAY

The first and best thing you can do when trying to find a mentor or discern if one is right for you is to ask the Holy Spirit! It might take longer than you anticipate, or the answer might be different than what you'd expect, but He will answer you.

Recently a new member of my Bible study shared that she prayed for a mentor for quite a while, yet felt like nothing was happening. Oftentimes, when it feels like nothing is happening, everything is happening. She prayed, let the people around her know she was looking for a mentor, and eventually was told about my Bible study! She wound up being incredibly grateful that she was patient and waited upon the Lord.

James 1:5 tells us, "But if any of you lacks wisdom, let him ask of God, who gives to all generously and without reproach, and it will be given to him."

Are you looking for a mentor? Pray! Ask God for wisdom.

2. EXAMINE THE FRUIT

I've had people ask for access to myself or my circle who personally had no evidence of the results they promised. If I don't see that in their own life, I will proceed cautiously. Do your due diligence to observe the fruit of your prospective mentors or influencers. Are their fruits what you want in your life? Are you seeing people changed by their influence for the better? Are you seeing a healthy lifestyle? Are you seeing them exemplify the character of Jesus?

"You will know them by their fruits. Grapes are not gathered from thorn bushes, nor figs from thistles, are they? So every good tree bears good fruit, but the bad tree bears bad fruit. A good tree cannot bear bad fruit, nor can a bad tree bear good fruit. Every tree that does not bear good fruit is cut down and thrown into the fire. So then, you will know them by their fruits." (Matthew 7: 16-20)

3. ASK FOR TESTIMONY
Interviewing people that have been influenced, either directly or indirectly, by someone you'd like to learn from is a great way to investigate if that mentor is a good fit for you! Don't just rely on the referrals the potential mentor gives you; do your research. Your time and energy are valuable, so don't waste them.

START WITH YOUR INNER CIRCLE

In Section Three, we'll explore more closely the different areas of your life in which you can be mentored. For instance, a business mentor is probably not the best mentor for your health, finances, or marriage. Depending on your circumstances, you may want more than one mentor for different areas of your life.

For starters, one of the best ways for continuous mentoring—along with Scripture and the Holy Spirit—is your inner circle. You've probably heard them many times, but these quotes bear repeating: "You're the average of the five people you spend the most time with" and "show me your friends and I'll show you your future." While these quotes sound like clichés, I know them to be true. Any parent of a teenager knows this for *certain*. When there's a change in a child's behavior or attitude, it can often be traced to their circle of friends.

Think back on your own life and take inventory of your progression. How did your circle of friends influence you? As you changed that circle, you likely changed as well—hopefully, for the better. Furthermore, as you reflect on different stages in your life, take note of who your circles of friends were. You were probably friends because you were all comfortable together. Why? Because you had common ground. Maybe it was because you played sports, or you had the same passion for technology. Whatever it was that bonded you together, you were what the Bible calls "equally yoked"!

But back to the current moment: it's important to audit the people around you. Make sure that you're spending time with people who are in line with what you want for your own life. Rita Davenport says, "Don't hang around people more messed up than you!" and "Never be the smartest person in the room." If you want to be successful in your business, find people who are further along than you. If you want to grow in intimacy with God, then find people who are madly in love with Him. Surround yourself with people you admire and want to learn from. There are a few important principles to keep in mind when thinking about relationships, the first of which is levels of access.

LEVELS OF ACCESS

While you can count dozens, even hundreds of people as your friends, your inner circle should only be around five or six people. These are the people who are not only your most trusted confidants, but those who will also love and respect you enough to give critical feedback. They will speak the truth in love. While bigger seems to always be better, you'll be surprised how much more valuable you'll become to your larger circle (community) when you carefully curate your most trusted inner circle. Limit your inner circle to the *irons* in your life—those who sharpen you, and you, them.

"As iron sharpens iron, so one person sharpens another." (Proverbs 27:17)

It's important to utilize several levels of access. Outside your inner circle is another circle with about 10-20 people. These are also like-minded friends that you interact with, but not as often, nor with intimate details of your life. See where this is going? You'll continue this process as each circle widens to more people with less access to you. Not everyone is going to be someone you pick up the phone for in the middle of the night, nor is everyone someone you would call for advice on something personal.

Throughout your life, people will move in and out of your circles. It's not like you say, "Hey you, move to the next circle!" or "Sorry buddy, you are in my outer circle now!" That is *not* the concept. This is an organic process that sometimes won't involve conversations with the other person. You'll know when you need to move someone out to protect yourself, and you'll know when someone is safe enough to bring in.

You will not only learn and grow from the relationships in your inner circle, but you'll discover a rewarding and rich flow of knowledge and discipleship as you pour into each other. That's right: your inner circle does not exist for them to merely pour into you, it's for you to pour into *each other*. This should be an environment with a desire to grow in every area of your life. Think about it; if each person in your inner circle is committed to their growth *and* yours, it will be a rich resource for mentorship!

In his book *7 Habits of Highly Effective People*, the late Stephen Covey shares a relationship concept called "emotional bank accounts." Similar to financial bank accounts, people make deposits and withdrawals from each other. Some examples of making deposits with people (or reducing withdrawals) are caring, keeping commitments, clarifying expectations, paying attention to the little things, showing personal integrity, and apologizing when we make a withdrawal.

When deposit levels are high, communication and trust levels flow almost effortlessly. If a relationship is overdrawn, the relationship is in jeopardy.

Recently, a family member shared how a friendship quickly became exhausting because the only time she heard from her friend was when they wanted or needed something. It was a pattern, not an incident. Wisely, she gently moved that friend to the outer circle of her relationships. Make it a habit to deposit into the people around you and surround yourself with people who do the same.

ALIGNED MENTORSHIP

Seeking mentorship is generally associated with the desire to grow and get better in a certain area (or areas) of your life. That's a good thing! However, people often remain stuck in a rut because they fear failure or they justify why they don't need to grow. In his book "The Gap and the Gain," Dan Sullivan instructs his readers to focus on the positive *gain* and measuring their progress from where they've been to where they are instead of the *gap* of disappointment if they've fallen short. Reflect on your own life. What gains have you made in your journey?

In order to continue to move forward and achieve more of these gains, it's important to set goals for what you want out of mentorship rather than just winging it. Set goals that are aligned with who you are and whom you want to become; where you are today and the gain of where you want to be in your future. I call this process "alignment goal setting."

Alignment goal setting is confirming your goals are aligned with your core values. It's important to set goals based on what God is speaking into your heart—what His best is for you. For example, it's important to remember that God's design for us is different than the world's. In her book "Grace over Grind," author Shae Bynes shares that God's desire for us is *not* to hustle and grind as global society teaches but to instead live in gratitude and grace. When we are aligned with God's plan for our lives, we experience a rhythm of rest and balance that is much more desirable than the workaholic, burn-the-candle-at-both-ends lifestyle. Doesn't that sound like a wonderful way to work and live?

Another beautiful truth of God's design for our lives is that He has the power to exceed your wildest dreams. If you're careful to make God the *source* of your mentorship and goal setting, everything else will be a resource for your success. This is exciting because traditional goal setting tells you to set a goal that is believable and achievable. What if you knew that God could perform miracles in your life that are *unbelievable*? It is possible!

Ephesians 3:20-21 says, "Now to Him who is able to do far more abundantly beyond all that we ask or think, according to the power that works within us, to Him be the glory in the church and in Christ Jesus to all generations forever and ever. Amen."

Thomas just experienced this. He had been praying for a supernatural miracle in his business and went through a season of trials and setbacks. Along with staying consistent in prayer, he was diligent in aligning his goal setting and activities with God's purpose and design for his life. After a period of time that felt like nothing was happening, *everything* happened! He leaned into supernatural overdrive and achieved a success level that no one thought was possible. Since he worked quietly and diligently without broadcasting hype on social media, many thought it was a sudden, overnight success story. In reality, it was just the tip of the iceberg that they saw, not the hard work that built the foundation. Thomas and I believe in under-promising and over-delivering.

Don't limit your goals to what *you* believe is possible, but what *God* says is possible.

Another important aspect of aligned goal setting and choosing a mentor accordingly is not to compare yourself to others. Align your mentors and goals with what is authentically best for *you*. In my business, I do a strategy session with people who are just starting out as entrepreneurs. Instead of laying out what I think they should do, I simply ask the question, "What do *you* want? What are your dreams, desires, and discontents?" Then we craft a business plan that fits what they desire and want to achieve and what lifestyle they want to lead.

Lastly, make your goal-setting personal. Talk it over with your spouse and family. Make it an "our goal" not a "my goal." Not only will your goals dictate who mentors you, you can also use your mentor to help hold you accountable to those goals that are aligned with your values. You will experience a sense of peace and harmony when your goals are aligned with your mentor and those who coach and influence you.

I like to use the following goal setting process:

PLAN > DO > ASSESS > ADJUST > CELEBRATE > REPEAT

Make your plan, get into activity, assess your results, make adjustments, celebrate, then repeat!

This simple goal-setting exercise, when done consistently, gets easier and becomes a habit. It's important to set aside time to not only work your plan, but to check on your progress. This is where mentorship comes in. As I touched on earlier, it's wise to have an accountability partner or mentor to help you stay on track. When you make a habit of aligned goal setting, you'll also be setting an example for those around you, like your children, business associates, and mentees. Aligned mentorship and goal setting is duplicatable. When you fish, you want to teach others to fish; not fish for them.

This is the basis of mentorship: The mentor doesn't do the work *for* the mentee, but teaches them by example and brings them into it. Which brings us to a shift in this chapter: we'll explore a few principles you can use as someone who mentors others and carries influence.

PROTECT YOUR ACCESS

In his book "The Power of One More," Ed Mylett shares that you can't change or control other people, but you *can* change the level of access people have to you. He shares, "If people choose to think and do things that are counterproductive to your living your best life, then it's incumbent on you to make the choices that best serve you."

It's OK to protect your access, regardless of whether you're in the public eye or not. It's important to give yourself permission to do so. Ask God for discernment to help you determine the access other people have based on aligned values, goals, standards, and desired outcomes.

In my business, I often have speakers and trainers reaching out and asking to have access to me and my organization. I have hundreds of thousands of independent entrepreneurs in my network, so for many, they see a gold mine—*if* they can tap into it. I have a very short list of outside trainers I allow to have access to my team. Focus is key, so an unvetted message can be a huge distraction, especially if it's a message that contradicts our core values and training systems. While I'm always open to meeting people and learning new concepts, I still make sure to take the time to vet the content. The same should be applied when you are introducing mentorship into your life. It is crucial to learn to protect your access. In fact, being diligent and creating habits to protect your access will help you stay peaceful and productive.

Here are some tips to do so:

LIMIT YOUR PINGS

You don't have to open or answer every "ping" you receive. There are numerous ways for people to reach out to you, including email, phone, text, messenger, Voxer, WhatsApp, a simple knock at your door, and more. Each of these is what I would consider a "ping."

One way of protecting your access is to limit the ways you ping or accept pings. For instance, I have a mentor who will only accept messages by email or text. He sets a clear boundary to protect his access. It also makes his life easier! I do not have voicemail on my landline or my cell phone. My greeting simply asks the caller to email or text me instead. This is also helpful because, with my travel schedule, I can often be in a time zone that is 10 hours different from the caller!

LIMIT YOUR AVAILABILITY

You may feel like you are on-call 24 hours a day, especially if you are an entrepreneur. Worse yet, others think you are as well!

However, you teach people how to treat you. Setting times for your availability is not only healthy, but it sets a great example for boundaries. Clear boundaries also create less stress in your life, and create room for rhythm and rest. You cannot pour from an empty cup.

Putting autoresponders in place or hiring an assistant to screen your messages can be very helpful. Again, just because someone reaches out, especially a stranger or solicitor, doesn't require a response. Think of it like your own personal spam folder.

LEARN HOW TO PLAY "TENNIS"

I recently had a leader tell me how exhausted she was from answering all the questions and requests that came to her. After some coaching, she discovered she had no boundaries, and felt responsible to answer and fix everything that came her way. So, she learned to play "tennis."

What I mean by that is, just like the game of tennis, when someone serves you the ball, you lob it back. An example of playing this kind of tennis is answering a question with, "If you weren't able to reach me, how would you have found this answer?" Empower people to resolve their issues. Sometimes it's easier for them to ask you than to do their own research. You teach people how to treat you, so lob the ball back to them and play some tennis!

UTILIZE THE 4 D'S

I often use a system called the 4 D's to sort through the pings I receive. The 4 D's are:

1. Do it
2. Delegate it
3. Delay it
4. Dump it

Learn to sort requests and projects into these four categories. When you get a ping, ask yourself, "what is the best response?" Is it something that is of value and that you need to do? Often the best way to avoid procrastination is to just get it done. Then **DO IT**.

Is it something you must do, or is it something you can delegate? If you can, **DELEGATE IT**.

Is it something you need to do, but not of urgency? Then **DELAY IT**... but you must create a plan as to when you will come back to it.

Is it something you can say "no" to? Then simply **DUMP IT**.

Create a system for sorting your requests; don't leave them to clutter your brain. Put it down on paper or your favorite digital organizational system. I love crossing things off my to-do list!

JUST START!

Have you ever procrastinated on a project because you wanted it to be perfect? In our journey of being mentored and mentoring others, the idea of "progress, not perfection" is crucial. Just like the story about Lori not wanting to read the Bible because it was too overwhelming to start, it's easy to put off seeking mentors or mentoring others because it's not black and white.

But I'm telling you: Just start! As you go, however, it's important to celebrate smaller achievements and not just the end goal. Eventually, this helps us accept and enjoy things even if they aren't perfect because we can recognize evidence of our progress. With *progress* as your focus and celebrating the wins, you can let go of the unrealistic expectation of being perfect and simply put one foot in front of the other.

Joe Calloway, author of "Be the Best at What Matters Most" said, "Imperfect progress is better than perfect stagnation."

Before we move on to the next section, it's time to surrender and let God lead your way. With a strong foundation of knowing who you are and who Jesus is, you can confidently seek the sources of mentorship available to you through Scripture, Holy Spirit, and people. Seek this guidance for your life on a consistent basis, and you will grow in every area. Place God first and trust the plans He has for you, and keep that three-stranded cord intact.

"But seek first His kingdom and His righteousness, and all these things will be provided to you." (Matthew 6:33)

Jesus is *my* primary mentor. Will you make Him yours? He will speak to you through Scripture, Holy Spirit, and the people that He places in your path along life's journey. He will guide you and lead you in His will and His perfect plans to help you prosper in every area of your life.

Water Walker Reflections:

In your life, write down the percentage you are mentored in each area, totaling 100:
(Example: Scripture 40%, Holy Spirit 30%, People 30%)
Scripture _____
Holy Spirit _____
People who Influence/Mentor me: _____
If needed, create an action plan for re-adjusting these percentages: _____
_____
_____

In protecting your access, which areas do you need to work on the most? *(1-5 with 1 being the area you need to work on the most and 5 the least)*

Limit Your Pings _____

Limit Your Availability _____

Learn to Play Tennis _____

Create Filters _____

The 4 D's _____

Write down a few action steps to better protect your access in each of these areas: _____

_____

_____

_____

_____

Start today with the 4 D's. Write out a list of all the activities and requests you are currently experiencing, then filter them. Which ones can you:

DO: _____

DELEGATE: _____

DELAY: _____

DUMP: _____

Who are the inner circle "irons" in your life?

1) _____ 2) _____

3) _____ 4) _____ 5) _____

What area of discerning who influences you can you utilize more: prayer, examining fruit, or testimony? _____

_____

_____

_____

_____

Describe the attributes of your Inner Circle: _____
_____
_____
_____

With "progress over perfection" as your focus, what can you surrender to let God move more in your life? _____
_____
_____
_____

What is an area in your life you've made progress in that you can celebrate? _____
_____
_____
_____

Ripple Effect:

How is what you learned in this chapter going to affect those around you? _____
_____
_____
_____
_____

MENTOR LIKE JESUS IN EVERY AREA OF YOUR LIFE

Chapter 8

LIVING IN BALANCE

NOW THAT WE'VE covered the *why*, *how*, and *who* of mentorship in the previous two sections, we'll cover the *what* as we move into the next. Section one laid the foundation of who you are and why it matters. In section two, we explored how we are mentored through Scripture, Holy Spirit, and people. In section three, we'll look specifically at each part of our life circle—home, work, and community—and how we can apply mentorship principles to each area. As I've often said, "how we do anything is how we do everything," so approaching each of these areas with a healthy template (like a blueprint for construction) will assist with the decisions we make and the direction we'll go to achieve the success we desire.

Now, let's jump into the application of mentorship. What does that look like? How do we apply, with purpose, mentorship in all we do? Well, to begin, I want to start with a few questions that will shape how we move forward. I want you to ask yourself:

- What is my identity?
- What fruit am I currently producing, and what fruit do I *want* to bear?
- What is my current impact, and what impact would I like to be making?
- What is the legacy I am leaving?

Now, let's take a look at each of these areas a bit more in-depth.

IDENTITY: Now that you've (hopefully) got yourself tethered to God's anchor, building a strong understanding of *who* you are, *why* you are here, and *how* you are mentored, you can look ahead to how you'll move forward. A key question to ask at this point is, "What do you stand for?" The answer to this question will shape everything that happens next.

In their business book "Change the Culture, Change the Game," Roger Connors and Tom Smith establish a concept for business success: Experiences promote beliefs, beliefs impact actions, and actions generate results. Their theory is that if you want to generate positive results, you must start at the beginning with experiences, or simply put, "life happenings." Your *experiences* create your identity, which affects your *beliefs*, which impact your *actions*, which then generate your *results*. Your identity affects everything in your life; from your family to your relationships, from your workplace to your community. It affects how you will be mentored, and it affects how you will mentor others.

FRUIT: What kind of fruit do you want to bear as you pursue and live out mentorship? *Fruit* is the outward actions that result from the inward condition of a person's heart—of our identity. As the Holy Spirit sanctifies us, we become more like Jesus and, in turn, bear fruit like healthier relationships, bringing people to the saving knowledge of Christ, and helping those around us create healthy habits and more deeply understand the Word. We can't do this on our own, with our own strength, but rather through Jesus in us. Intentionally growing in our walk with Christ, inviting the Holy Spirit to transform us, and actively obeying God in all He calls us to do is a continual, consistent process that will reap endless benefits, including fruit. However, fruit grows through abiding, not striving. Are you abiding in God, being mentored through His Word and Spirit?

IMPACT: You can make the world a better place through the way you live your life. So, what impact will you make in your home, community, and workplace? No matter your status, job title, or age, you can make an impact on the world around you. You've likely heard the following saying before, but it bears repeating: *God doesn't call the qualified; he qualifies the called.* When you continually look to Him for wisdom, guidance, and power, He will work through you in all you do: your relationships, home, neighborhood, workplace... everywhere you go! Thinking about the impact you want to leave on the world around you not only influences how you choose others to mentor you, but also how you mentor others. Your current *impact* will affect your future *legacy!*

LEGACY: What legacy will you leave behind after you're gone? Usually, the first thought many have when hearing the word "legacy" is about money or inheritance. However, that couldn't be further from the truth. It's not material items that make up your legacy; it's who you are as a person. What healthy values and character are you developing and demonstrating to leave a mark on the world? What will you be known for?

Furthermore, your work/life balance will be revealed in your legacy. At your funeral, who will want to speak about the powerful impact your mentorship has made? If your business associates rush the microphone, but your family chooses to be silent because they have nothing to say (as was the case with my father), you're in trouble. The good news is, if you ponder this thought and are not happy with it, you can still do something about it. You can make changes.

I always loved the movie "A Christmas Carol," where mean-spirited, selfish Ebenezer Scrooge is visited by the ghosts of Christmas Past, Present and Future. Terrified by the error of his ways, he wakes on Christmas Day a changed man full of the joy of Christmas.

One of Ed Mylett's most inspiring stories is about the powerful transformation of his father. An alcoholic his entire life, Ed's father was confronted with an ultimatum from Ed's mother to make the change or leave. His father made that change. In his book, Ed wrote, "The greatest gift my dad gave our family was loving us all enough to find the strength and courage to get sober over 30 years ago. This changed our family tree forever."

The late founder of my company, Norwegian Petter Morck, shared this statement with me over 30 years ago: "Your legacy will affect many generations."

Petter was a visionary and understood that the seeds we plant through simply being who we are and the way we live will impact our culture—our families, our businesses, and the people around us on a daily basis. This culture, over time, will reveal our legacy, not only as a company or as entrepreneurs but, most importantly, as people.

So, what legacy will you leave? Your answer will tell you a lot about your priorities, and what may need to shift.

HOW'S YOUR QUALITY OF LIFE?

I want to pause for a moment before we move on. I know we've been covering a lot of ground so far, and it can be overwhelming. You may be asking, "So, where do we go from here? How do I apply these mentorship principles to my life?" While we may not be able to do "everything," but we can do "something" by taking little steps. Here's a tool I discovered years ago that I use to gain congruency in every area of my life. I call it:

"Do the right thing, in the right way, for the right reason."

I apply this formula of sorts when faced with a decision. Is it the right thing, in the right way, for the right reason? Sometimes you have the right reason, but perhaps the wrong thing or the wrong way. Or maybe you are doing the right thing, but in the wrong way. By filtering your decisions and actions through this principle, you can stay in alignment. However, it's important to apply this in every area of your life. What good is it to be known as a success in the marketplace but a failure at home, with your relationships, or in community?

My friend and mentor, Mark Fournier, founder of "Limitless Coach," developed a life quotient test called LQ. You've likely heard of IQ (intelligence quotient), and EQ (emotional quotient), which measure your aptitude in areas of mental and emotional capacity. However, Mark developed a way of measuring your aptitude regarding your level of happiness and fulfillment: your *quality* of life. You can think of LQ as standing for *life quality*.

To begin thinking about the balance in your life and your LQ, create a balance wheel like the one below. On a scale of 0 to 10, rate each of the areas of your life shown around the wheel, with 0 being the *least* satisfying, and 10 being the *most* satisfying. Be as honest as you possibly can. Then place a dot at the number that corresponds with your score and then connect the dots all the way around the wheel.

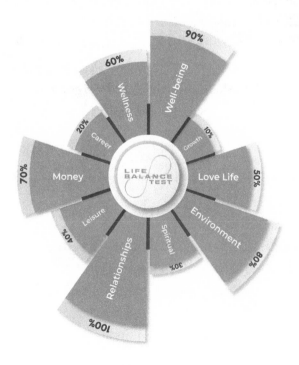

The main idea behind the balance wheel is this: If your life was a wheel like the tires on your car, how smoothly would it roll? Would you have flat spots that might not roll at all, or would it roll effortlessly due to a lack of dips and flat areas? By the way, although a bigger wheel (resulting from higher scores) might be appealing, just remember, a small round wheel will roll far more smoothly than a large flat one.

So, if you've identified your flat areas, where do you start in the process of balancing your LQ wheel? I'd suggest beginning your work on the lowest three areas (even at the expense of those with the highest scores, which might temporarily lower slightly as a result).

Once you have achieved greater balance, you can then attempt to continue raising them all to keep from becoming complacent and dissatisfied with your life once you adjust to your new scores. However, it's important to note that no one can ever get a perfect work/life balance. The goal is to simply smooth things out and change your priorities accordingly.

Additionally, Mark has provided a QR code to take the test, if you prefer to do it digitally. You can find it by scanning the code with your phone camera:

MARK FOURNIER PRESENTS:

TAKE THE TEST NOW! IT'S 'FREE, FUN, FAST, & EASY'!

Life Balance Test is a fast, fun, and easy self-assessment that allows you to measure (and ultimately improve) the quality of your life (your LQ / Life Quotient) by helping you understand and visualize where your life is in (and out of) balance. We've divided your life into 10 separate categories listed in this graphic and then created an app that allows you to assign a value to each category. Once you're done, the app will factor in your scores along with the degree of balance in your life from one category to the next, to determine your LQ. The more balanced your life, the higher your LQ score will be.

Just aim the camera on your phone at the following QR Code and it will take you to the app, where you will know your personal LQ within 2 minutes, along with ways to improve your balance, and your score!

WWW.LIMITLESSU.NET

PRIORITIZE THROUGH ASKING QUESTIONS

"Nobody's life is perfectly balanced. It's a conscious decision to choose your priorities every day."

—Elizabeth Hasselbeck

We are all given the same 24 hours each day. How we decide to use and divide this time can mean the difference between a hectic schedule that leaves us wondering where the day went, or a peacefully ordered schedule with rhythm and rest. So, how do you make better choices about priorities? In this case, the quality of your life can be directly traced to the quality of the questions you ask. Whether it's regarding your home, relationships, workplace or community, a simple litmus test can be applied.

Ask yourself the following questions while filtering through priorities:

- Is it healthy?
- Does it bless others?
- Does it move me forward in God's purpose and plan for my life?
- Is this God's will?

Protecting your energy and time starts with choosing the activities that are aligned with these questions.

For example, I personally don't watch television. I've heard it said that television is "tell a vision." I am not interested in a box telling me my vision. I have no idea about the life of the Kardashians or who the latest *Bachelor* is. I believe that God has called us to create the story of our own life, and not be caught up and hypnotized in other people's lives. If I were to ask myself the four questions above, I would quickly find the answers to be a resounding "no!" It is not healthy, it doesn't bless others, it doesn't move me forward, and thus is not God's will. Therefore, I can deduce that watching television is not aligned with the way I want to live. In addition to the questions above, you can go back to the 4 D's we learned in the previous chapter: Do it, Delegate it, Delay it, or Dump it. First, is this something you *want* to do? Can you *delegate* it to someone else? Can it be *delayed?* Or is it something you should *not* do? Let's explore how this looks when filtering through different requests made to us. If you say "yes" to every request without thinking it through or asking these key questions, you can quickly end up overwhelmed. However, even more importantly, you can also get off track from God's will. Recently, my friend Jennifer was asked to participate in one of the activities at her son's school. While she has three preschoolers at home and works remotely, she simply asked for time to pray and seek guidance before she gave an answer. (I encourage you to make a habit of this yourself and not always jump into a quick yes or no answer.) Jennifer took the request through the 4 D's, and her answer was "yes." Through prayer, she was reminded that more than ever, now is the time when parents need to be in the school observing and influencing—not just turning it over to someone else to instruct our children. While she had to create time in her home and business schedule to say "yes," she saw it as a priority and a confirmation to do the right thing, in the right way, for the right reason. In this example, Jennifer initially *delayed* her answer before she agreed, as it aligned with her values. Answering these questions and saying "no" to a conversation or task that is not in your sphere of influence frees up more time and energy to do those things that *are* important. I call it the

Law of the Vacuum. When you're so busy dealing with every-thing served up to you (think back to that tennis analogy), you don't have the space or capacity to filter down your priorities. Clearing out ineffective conversations and tasks allows you to fill that space with things you should be doing. For example, I do my best not to get caught up in gossip. It's not only a waste of time, it's also destructive. I'm grateful that my inner circle of friends also resists this temptation. I've literally been in a con-versation with a friend in my inner circle who stopped and said, "This is gossip, and we should have nothing to do with this."

SPHERES OF INFLUENCE

Another key component of staying in balance is addressing your spheres of influence:

- Inner Circle: Areas within your control
- Middle Circle: Areas you can influence
- Outer Circle: Everything else

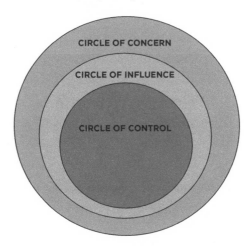

Our inner circle is not about controlling other people but rather activities and decisions we personally experience, like our schedules, how we treat our families, and what we put in our bodies. Our middle circle of influence includes areas of concern we have access to and the ability to act on or speak to, such as issues at work or conflict between our kids. It's healthy to stay in your inner circles of control and influence. While we can always have concern and pray over things we can't control in our outer circle, it should contain things we do not *worry* about, such as global issues.

Matthew 6:34 says, "So do not worry about tomorrow; for tomorrow will worry about itself. Each day has enough trouble of its own." Though we might be concerned with a certain situation or area, we are to give our worries to God. He cares, He is working, and He walks through it *with* us.

My mom is a big worrier, so we have a fun interaction where I share a worry quote with her. It always makes her laugh with a promise to worry less. A couple of my favorites:

"Worrying is a bad use of the imagination."

"Worrying is like a rocking chair; it gives you something to do, but it doesn't get you anywhere."

"Worry is the absence of Faith."

> **"Worrying is like praying for
> something you do not want."
> —Sharon Lechter**

Now, this does not mean that we can't *act* on areas out of our control. If God calls you to move into an area of your concern to make a difference, then you definitely should be obedient!

The problem comes when this is your *focus* without any plan for resolution. This is when it becomes a worry that is not healthy. I am inspired by those whom God has called to step into a calling to effect change and inspire and strengthen the courage of others. In our final chapters, I'll be sharing inspiring stories of world changers such as Harriet Tubman and William Wilberforce. They found ways to replace worry with courage and action, effecting change on a large (and even global) level. Fruit grows through abiding, not striving! It's all in the balance, like the Serenity Prayer:

> *God grant me the serenity*
> *To accept the things I cannot change,*
> *Courage to change the things I can, and*
> *Wisdom to know the difference.*

Part of knowing the difference is found in those four areas we talked about at the beginning of the chapter: identity, fruit, impact, and legacy. What kind of impact do you want to make? As we'll explore in the following chapters, we'll see that there are a number of cultural spheres (mountains) that desperately need people called to make a difference in. Are you one of these people? God is calling a wave of Water Walkers!

THE SEVEN MOUNTAINS

In 1975, Bill Bright, founder of Campus Crusade, and Loren Cunningham, founder of Youth with a Mission (YWAM), had a historic meeting in Colorado at which God gave them a concept called "seven mountains." Currently, two of my mentors,

Lance Wallnau and Johnny Enlow, carry their vision forward and lead this movement to affect today's culture. The core of the message is if we are to make an impact, then we have to affect the seven spheres, or mountains, of society that are the pillars.

These seven mountains are:

- Business
- Government
- Media
- Arts and Entertainment
- Education
- Family
- Religion

In essence, God told these four agents of change where the location of the battlefield lies. It is here where culture will be won or lost. Satan has been busy for many generations, as he's quietly crept into each of these cultural mountains. If you look at each mountain, you'll easily see how it's been taken over by a message opposite to God's teaching. Each mountain's worldview is a reflection of the influence by those who operate at the top. The more ungodly the leadership of each mountain, the more ungodly the culture. However, the Godlier the leadership, the more righteous the culture, bearing the fruit of God's Spirit. Thus, it doesn't matter what the majority worldview is of each mountain; what matters is the leadership and who controls it.

What is your mountain(s) of influence? I encourage you to pray and ask God to show you ways to make an impact. We can't look around and hope that others will do it. If God calls you, accept your marching orders. So often, we look at the injustices in the world or the cultural battlefield and say, "I'll pray for that." But we need to put feet on those prayers!

In October 2018, at the invitation of Lance Wallnau, Thomas and I attended a unique gathering of these *mountains* in Washington, D.C. The National Renewal Summit united top government, business, and church leaders to collaborate and make an impact on society together. We invited our dear friend Bob Lenz, pastor and founder of Life Promotions Youth Ministry and Lifest, one of the largest Christian music festivals in the world. Bob is a leader in the religion mountain, while Thomas and I are leaders in the business mountain.

At this event, we learned the importance of not only speaking God's truth in our own sphere of influence, but to partner with other mountains. What we can't do alone, we can do together. There's power in partnerships.

Parents are rising up and getting involved in school boards, homeschooling, or choosing private education to take back the education mountain. Citizens who once had no interest in government are rising up to run for office and take back corrupt government mountains. Traditional mainstream media ratings are plummeting as people are tired of lies and turning to the truth to take over the media mountain. Corrupt church leaders are being exposed to clean out the religious mountain. God is blessing businesses that resist the cultural bullying to take back the business mountain. Families are looking up and, on their knees, praying to God for guidance as we take back the family mountain.

God is pouring out instruction for service to everyone, young and old, rich and poor, regardless of education or profession. Like this book God called me to write. I could have shrugged it off and made excuses for why I would not be obedient. He was clear that he didn't want me to delay, delegate, or dump it; He called me to *do it*. It aligned with my identity, fruit, impact, and legacy.

WHAT DO YOU WANT TO BE KNOWN FOR?

In his book, "Know What You're For," author Jeff Henderson challenges his readers to ask great questions about *what* and *who* you are for; whether you're a stay-at-home parent, an athlete or a CEO, you have many choices to make on a daily basis. As I've shared many times thus far, when you have a firm foundation and purpose for your life, you'll choose wisely and say "yes" to the opportunities that will lead you in the right direction. On the flip side, when you don't know your purpose or the direction you're going, any path will do. Nothing creates balance in your life like knowing what you stand for.

Often, whether it's our personal life, business or community, we tend to make it all about *us*. This is a very narcissistic approach to life. Instead, ask yourself, "Who am I for?" When God is the center of your life, that answer is easy: We are for God and His will for our lives, which includes being of service and witness to others. With this as our starting point, we will know what we are for.

Jeff closes his book by asking his readers to ponder these two questions:

- "What do you *want* to be known for?"
- "What *are* you known for?"

The first question is about what we desire, wish, and hope for. The second question is what we are known for in reality. Think back to the questions at the beginning of this chapter. What fruit do we bear? What impact are we leaving on the world?

The difference between the two questions Jeff poses is *action*. We may *want* or *desire* a certain outcome in our lives, but until we get into the *activity* necessary to accomplish it, nothing will happen. People don't listen to what you *say*; they listen to what you *do*, for actions speak louder than words. If results happened because we *say* we want something to be so, we'd all be healthy, wealthy, and happy.

This brings us back to the point of this book, and specifically to this chapter on balance in every area of your life. Balance isn't achieved by simply *saying* we want balance; it's consciously making choices that reflect our values and acting on them. In other words, "walk your talk." I encourage you to journal your thoughts and ideas and make a plan to live each area of your life in full alignment with your values. Living a life in balance with joy and congruency happens when everything is in alignment with our identity. Oh, to be satisfied with our thoughts, words, and actions, which ultimately lead to our results, impact, and legacy.

"The fruit of a person's mouth [words] will be satisfied; He will be satisfied with the product of his lips." (Proverbs 18:20)

Ask yourself great questions. The future is a blank page on which you get to write your answer. Your life is your story; write it well and edit often.

Water Walker Reflections:

What fruit do you want to bear?

_____

_____

_____

What impact would you like to make in your home, community, and workplace?

_____

_____

_____

When you follow through and do what you say you will do, what legacy will you leave?

_____

_____

_____

What are some requests you can say "no" to that could be taking you away from saying "yes" to something more aligned with your values?

_____

_____

_____

What is your mountain(s) of influence? _____

_____

_____

What are some ways to impact your circle of control & influence?

_____

_____

_____

What are some areas of concern you've given too much of your time and worry to? _____
_____
_____
_____

Ripple Effect:

Pray and ask God to show you ways that you can use your influence to make an impact. What actions will you take today to put feet to those prayers? _____
_____
_____
_____

Who can you reach out to and ask to hold you accountable?
_____
_____
_____

How will living your life in balance aligned with your values make an impact on those around you? _____
_____
_____
_____

Chapter 9

YOUR STORY BEGINS AT HOME

"If you want to change the world, go home and love your family."

—Mother Teresa

AS WE SEEK out mentorship and mentoring others, it must begin at home. In this chapter, we'll talk about how mentorship plays out in our marriages and raising children—those directly in our homes. However, in order to pour into the people in our home, we must first tend to ourselves. After all, you can't pour from an empty cup. Much like the instructions given during takeoff of an airplane, we reach for *our* oxygen mask first before assisting others.

So, let's start with you and your physical body. Remember: As a believer, your body is a *home* for Holy Spirit. It's good to make sure it's in good shape, well-kept, and regularly maintained, just like the house you live in. How many homes have you lived in in your lifetime? Unlike your house, you can't replace your body. Your body is the only one you have for the entirety of your life, so you must treat it accordingly!

So, how exactly do you treat your body as a home for Holy Spirit? Here are five practical ways you can start.

RESPECT YOUR BODY: As we've touched on quite a bit throughout this book, the Bible says that your body is a temple. We are to honor and respect our bodies as vessels! I'm grateful the profession I am in is centered around health and wellness. I learned to start taking care of my body and skin—even before signs of aging—out of respect for it. The products I work with are botanically based, made of good things from the earth. I like to call it salad or nutrition for your body!

FUEL YOUR BODY: The products you put on your skin and what you eat, drink, and take into your body are either fuel or poison—the choice is yours. In my business, we mentor people by helping them with their nutrition and fitness goals through our 30-Day Challenge. However, the key is that we don't focus on *just* 30 days; we teach the importance of getting into a *habit,* which starts shifting our choices. Once people start to experience renewed energy, clarity, and overall improvement of wellbeing, it is often much easier to continue their path of healthy living by implementing choices every day to *fuel* their bodies instead of poisoning them.

MOVE YOUR BODY: Another key in treating your body right is to get in the habit of exercising consistently, regardless of your age. This habit can truly be as simple as walking and stretching every day. One of the tricks I've learned is to put on exercise clothing first thing in the morning. Since I work from home and build my business around my life, I make sure that I fit in my workout routine. By being dressed and ready, it helps hold me accountable. I have a personal trainer I work with both in-person and virtually when I travel. If this isn't possible for you, it could be as easy as finding a workout buddy to keep you accountable, or even jumping on an online program or app.

STRENGTHEN YOUR BODY: No matter how old you are, it's an important practice to incorporate some sort of strength training—especially core work. My mom was 60 when my twins were born. If she sat on the floor to play with Liv and Alex, she had a hard time getting up. This really stuck with me. I asked my trainer for tips, and she told me that one of the quickest ways our body fails is when we don't regularly engage our core. Strength training doesn't have to be intense! You can simply incorporate bodyweight exercises like planks, squats, lunges, and push-ups to get some movement in.

LOVE YOUR BODY: Lastly, it's important to remember to love your body—just the way God made it. No matter your age or circumstance, you add value to the world around you. It's time to embrace just who you are on the inside *and* the skin you're in. Stop listening to what the world thinks is beautiful, and listen to what God says about you! If you need a reminder, head back to Chapter 2!

When my grandson Jonah was living near us in Arizona, it was a couple of months before my 60th birthday. I was driving him to soccer practice, fresh out of my beauty day (facial, hair, and nails). To my surprise, the quiet teenager in the backseat suddenly declared, "Nanna, you look so pretty today!"

"Why, thank you, Jonah!"

Quickly shrugging off how mushy he thought that sounded, he said, "Well, don't forget you'll be 60 in June."

"You know what, Jonah? I'm so glad I'm going to be 60 in June. Because if I weren't going to have my birthday, I wouldn't be here!" Suddenly, it hit him. "Oh, you're right, Nanna!"

Let the inner beauty God created shine no matter your age. I like to rephrase "anti-aging" as "aging well." After all, to anti-age is to die!

"Age is an issue of mind over matter. If you don't mind, it doesn't matter."—Mark Twain

In addition to your body, you must keep your mind, soul, and spirit healthy:

MIND HEALTH: For the purpose of this point, let's think of mind health as taking care of our brain. Our mind is our faculty of thinking, reasoning, and applying knowledge. You can actively work to keep your mind healthy by engaging your brain with puzzles or games, reading, learning, engaging socially, and consistently getting a good night's sleep. Since dementia runs in my family, I also take herbs, hydrate, and detox to help keep my mind clear.

INNER HEALTH: When I say "inner health," I mean the health of our spirit—the "inner man," as the Word says—and our soul. The soul has been referred to as the "seat of our emotions," which is also sometimes translated in the Bible as "heart." Taking care of our soul health can include things like inner healing, trauma work, therapy, open communication, and healthy relationships. It is critical to tend to our emotions as part of filling our cup to pour out, as we can easily "leak" on the people we're mentoring if we're neglecting our hearts.

However, it is equally important not to neglect our spirit! Feeding your spirit includes time in the Word, prayer, worship, church gatherings, small groups—anything that encourages you in the Lord. As I've mentioned before, I have a special, oversized stuffed white chair in the corner of our bedroom surrounded by my Bible, books, paper, and pens. After my husband and I have our prayer and devotional time together, I go to my prayer corner to fellowship with God and refresh my spirit with renewed instruction and conversation.

But I don't just leave it in the corner; I continue to talk to God and pray throughout my day. We live on a remote, peaceful lake. One of my favorite things to do is go out on my paddleboard in the morning or sunset when the lake is like glass. Connecting with nature, grounding my feet in the earth or water, listening to the call of the loons and watching the eagles soar is rejuvenating for me.

Whatever it looks like for you, make sure you create habits to care for your inner health. Tending to your soul and spirit allows you to serve others from the overflow—including your spouse.

JUST AS CHRIST LOVED THE CHURCH

The institute of marriage is one of the first things God established after creation. Needless to say, the love between a husband and wife is one of the most intimate things anyone can experience. However, this goes far beyond romantic love, as marriage truly emulates Christ's love for the Bride—that is, us!

A note for the single (or dating/engaged/divorced/widowed) readers: This is also relevant for you, regardless of where you are on your life's journey. I was there too, and in a few pages, I will share a bit of my story of meeting and marrying Thomas. Marriage is one of the most beautiful illustrations of our relationship with God, and one of the greatest ways we can demonstrate this love is by the way we treat our spouses. I always sign a wedding card with "May your kindest words be to each other."

Earlier, we discussed the importance of your inner circle and how when those closest to you have similar goals and values, you are equally yoked. This is not only valuable wisdom but also built-in accountability. However, the closest member of your inner circle should always be your spouse. I can pray and share Scripture, stories, books, and music with everyone in my inner circle, but the *first* person I go to is my husband. He makes me feel more at home than our house. One of our favorite ways to end a conversation or leave goes something like this:

"Love you!" one of us says.

"Love you more," the other replies.

Which is met with a final "Impossible."

By no means, however, is any marriage perfect. I can annoy my husband as much as he annoys me at times! But that's what life and love are all about—choosing each other everyday. For better or worse. We have to learn to take things in stride and focus on joy and what's great. One of the things Thomas and I have both committed to is consistently making our relationship a priority and never taking it for granted. It's easy to get careless or drift. One tip that helps us is to clearly communicate our schedules, always making it a priority to have consistent quality time together. We both love to read, so we'll often sit together with soft music playing while we enjoy our books. We also make it a point to regularly go for walks together and have date nights. We focus on making deposits.

Working to build a successful marriage takes commitment, courage, strength, communication, and a great sense of humor. Most importantly, it takes a lifetime of prayer.

COULDN'T HE BE FROM THE SAME CONTINENT?!

As I hope you know by now, we serve a God who loves us unconditionally and never gives up. When we make mistakes— and we will—it is not the end! We confess, repent, and are always met with the grace of God. I didn't have a healthy example of marriage growing up, and when I found myself in a failing marriage, God met me with that grace.

And He knew exactly what I needed.

He knew I couldn't go it alone; I needed a mentor!

When I was at a place where I knew I needed more personalized guidance in the area of relationships, I hired a coach. Mark Fournier, a professional coach, helped me with developing a healthy mindset around relationships. As a single mom paralyzed by a failed marriage, he helped me set clear boundaries. He coached me to make two lists of non-negotiables:

1. Things I *wanted* in a relationship.
2. And things I *didn't* want. This felt like I was learning a new way to walk, move and dance. I was all left feet; a fish out of water. Seeking God's way, not my way. I was slowly embracing a new normal.

In 2009, I was asked by a friend from Norway to speak in Dubai for his company's leaders. It was there that I met and fell in love with my husband, who is from Sweden. *I guess I forgot to write in my non-negotiables to fall in love with someone on the same continent!* By establishing clear boundaries with the help of Mark, one of my non-negotiables was being equally yoked in marriage. According to Scripture, being equally yoked means that we are not to pursue a romantic relationship with non-believers, as they do not have a yoke covenant with Christ. So, two people who *are* believers that are in a relationship or marriage *are* equally yoked.

Not only is Thomas equally yoked, but he is my best friend; my greatest support; my biggest comfort; my truest smile; my deepest love, and my favorite forever. We've been through tests and trials that have only made us stronger in our commitment and faith. I am so grateful God blessed me with the gift of a God-centered marriage. Seeking guidance and mentorship made a difference, and I'm grateful that I wasn't afraid to ask for help to reach my goals.

Another life-changing concept that Mark taught me was understanding the hormonal process of love. People who bounce around from relationship to relationship because they *lost the feeling* can actually be controlled by their hormones. We have likely all experienced or observed a new couple who can't control the euphoric stage of togetherness. It's a hormone called dopamine, and that head-in-the-clouds feeling, that passionate love, lasts from 12 to 18 months, according to Rutgers anthropologist Helen Fisher. If things are going well, *Psychology Today* states that after about four years in a relationship, dopamine decreases, and attraction goes down and gets replaced by the hormones oxytocin and vasopressin, which create the desire to bond, affiliate with, and nurture your partner. This leads to a long-lasting, steady dose of harmony and contentment. When people don't understand this hormonal process, they often jump around from relationship to relationship to get another hit from this addictive chemical.

Why am I bringing this up? Because it's important to know that relationships take work. The initial dopamine hit will wear off, and it's at that point that you have to be willing to choose your partner every day, regardless of "feelings." As you make the commitment every day to pour into the most important person in your inner circle, you will reap dividends in the long run, and this commitment will bleed into the other areas of your life in which you will be pouring out.

And one of these areas is your children, should you have children in your marriage (or future marriage).

TRAINING UP YOUR CHILDREN

"The goal of parenting isn't to create perfect kids; it's to point our kids to a perfect God."

—Lindsey Bell

Having five children, including identical twins, has been one of the biggest blessings in my life. I am constantly in awe of how beautifully different each child is. Through my twins, it's become even more apparent that only God can create each person so uniquely and personally! Identical twins form when the egg splits. I believe that the spirit enters upon conception, so not only does the egg split, but so does the spirit. This could definitely explain the sometimes-unexplainable connection that happens between identical twins.

Once, when the twins were at university, Liv was on the floor of their apartment working on a project while Alex was riding her bike home from class. Suddenly, Liv jumped, and she knew something happened to Alex. Sure enough, Alex was hit by an out-of-control biker coming down the hill, not paying attention. She was not severely injured, but at that very moment, Liv *knew*.

Even still, they are unique in every way, as God took this miracle of one and made two! Even in the womb, they had distinct personalities. In fact, I named them by the way they moved around. I instructed the doctors and nurses during their delivery. "Feel here? That's Olivia; she gently moves around. Now feel there? That's Alexandra; she makes quick movements. Feel the difference?" They were astonished to notice their difference even in the womb.

Even though each child is uniquely different, if you have more than one, you will discover that your love for them is equal. After all, this is how God loves us! I tell my children all the time, even as adults, "I love you all equally. I don't have a favorite." They know this to be true, as I demonstrate it not just in my words but in my actions. If there's ever a dispute, I am the first to say, "I am not picking a side. I love you all, so let's figure this out together."

One of the core principles of mentorship is understanding that we are *all* on an imperfect journey. I get it wrong! You'll get it wrong. We all get it wrong. But we can continue to walk forward in the journey of parenting, which, most importantly, is training up our children in the way of the Lord.

Proverbs 22:6 says, "Train up a child in the way he should go, Even when he grows older he will not abandon it."

As a parent, it's easy to become borderline obsessive about every moment of our child's journey. After all, they are completely dependent on us as babies! However, little by little, from the time they wean and start eating solids to the day they move out of our houses, we give them roots and wings to grow *and* fly.

Throughout each life stage, we can do these four things for our children: love them, pray for them, teach them, and let them go.

LOVE THEM

Above all else, we are called to love our children as God loves us—unconditionally, without restraint, and even when they are disobedient. Just as God extends grace, so should we. God's love never wavers or changes—He loves us no matter what direction we go. So should it be said of us as we love our children.

Have they taken a different path or worldview than yours? *Love them.*
Have they cut you off from their lives? *Love them.*
No matter the question, the answer is the same: *Love them.*

Loving your children will be a cornerstone that they can count on throughout their entire lives. Be quick to forgive, don't hold grudges, look for what's best, and speak gently into every area of their lives.

PRAY FOR THEM

It is an honor to pray for your children while they don't have the words, understanding, or insight to pray for themselves. However, no matter their age, it is imperative to stand in the gap, always interceding, much like Holy Spirit prays for us:

"Now in the same way the Spirit also helps our weakness; for we do not know what to pray for as we should, but the Spirit Himself intercedes for *us* with groanings too deep for words; and He who searches the hearts knows what the mind of the Spirit is, because He intercedes for the saints according to *the will of* God." (Romans 8:26-27)

Prayer isn't a trite quick fix. But you will never regret investing time in praying for their salvation, their gifts and calling, and their future. Praying for your children will be a cornerstone they can count on for the rest of their days. Who knows, maybe one day you'll hear about how your prayers saved their lives.

TEACH THEM

One of the biggest mistakes I've seen parents make is doing things for their children that they should be doing for themselves. It's almost as if they are looking for a *parent medal.* That is *not* our job! Early in my career, I was on the receiving end of a powerful mentoring moment. I was a mom with three young children. Petter Morck sat down with me and told me that in Europe, success often skips a generation. He knew my humble upbringing. I received my cousin Maree's hand-me-down clothing, so spoiling my children with shopping seemed very tempting, since I missed out on that while I was growing up.

He counseled me to have my children pay for half of the things they wanted and to take on chores as they were growing up. My oldest, Nathaniel, was the first for us to try this out on. One summer, when he was nine years old, he wanted a trick bike. I told him that he needed to come up with half the money, so he did it! He worked hard mowing lawns to get that bike, and we still have it in the rafters of our garage as a reminder!

All my kids started doing their own laundry at age 12, along with their usual chores, including dishes, cooking, and cleaning. If they made messes, they cleaned them up. My children now do the same with their children, my grandchildren. My granddaughter Selah was recently visiting, and even though she's only four years old, she folded all the laundry from the dryer without me asking.

I recently had a friend I mentor complain that it feels like all she does is laundry. When I shared my strategy, she implemented it as well. She reported back to me, "Just like that, the clean clothes they used to take off and throw in the laundry when trying to decide what to wear suddenly got put away!" When Mom did all the laundry, they didn't care what landed on the floor. Now that *they* were responsible, they were more careful.

I also had my children pay for half of their college/university education. The agreement was that if they earned an academic or sports scholarship, it contributed toward their half. This gave them an incentive to not only earn their way, but also build up their self-esteem. All five of my children received their education this way, debt-free, by attaining scholarships and working. Could I afford to pay their entire tuition? Yes. Was that in their best interest? No.

It also helped them resist and push back from the narrative, "Oh, you're a rich kid, so everything is paid for." Many of my kids' friends that had either a full scholarship or parents who paid their tuition blew off their education, didn't show up for class, and felt entitled later on in life. Teaching a strong work ethic is one of the best lessons you can give your children.

Children are not born with an instruction manual. It takes time and energy to seek out mentorship—through Scripture, Holy Spirit, and other people—for successful parenting. But I promise you; it is worth it!

Will you be a perfect parent? *No!* Be transparent with the mistakes you make, even with your children. There's a saying, "God is watching; give Him a good show." Guess what? Your children are watching, too. They are watching you in your relationship with your spouse. Your daughters are learning how to be treated by a man, and your sons are learning how to treat a woman. They are watching you walk out your faith, pray, go about your life, and how you make choices. They are watching how you interact with others, set goals, handle setbacks, set boundaries, and manage your disappointments. These are all things *they* need to learn, so watching you is one of the best forms of instruction. More is caught than taught.

Make sure your children know there is *one person* who will always be there for them, no matter what. God is always that person, and we are called to do the same. Let that person also be you.

LET THEM GO

Now, before these words make you freak out and panic, you have to understand what I mean by letting go. You never let them go in your *heart*: loving them, praying for them, and teaching them. However, you will let them go in the physical sense. One of the most difficult tasks of a parent is letting your child walk out your doors to lead their own life. I often see parents cling to their children in a very unhealthy manner at this life stage. But what happens if you help a butterfly break free from its cocoon by breaking it to let it out? The butterfly dies. The butterfly must get strong on its own to survive.

Abraham set this example for us not to allow our children to become our idols. When God instructed him to sacrifice Isaac, his only beloved son, Abraham was obedient, yet God spared Isaac on that mountain. Raising your child well is hard but learning to let them go out into the world and prove you did your job well is even tougher.

Now, here is some more potentially hard truth. Your children are not your first priority. Your marriage is your sacred covenant for life and should always be your number one priority after God. This does not mean that your children's needs are unmet, but rather it paves the way for a healthy transition for your children to become independent adults. So often, parents don't want to let go. When I've mentored parents through this process, they often explain in great detail, why their children must come first, even when they are young adults. They build a case for why they have to be involved in every aspect of their life, just like they did when their child was young. It's almost as if they feel they are a failure if they don't. However, this isn't God's design, and when parents begin to realize that truth, a burden lifts off their shoulders as they begin letting go.

When my twin daughters were in high school, they were on the volleyball team. There's a tradition in high school sports where, during senior year, they put on a parent night to honor the senior players and their parents. After this special evening, my girls told me that some of their teammates shared how much they admired me as their mother. Liv and Alex were confused and asked why—their teammates' moms were at *every* volleyball event. In contrast, I was at most of their matches but not all of them. I would let my girls know if I had a speaking engagement or another commitment and that I couldn't be there. It was never big drama, dripping emotions, or apologizing. I simply communicated if I could be there or not. Their teammates explained, "We are so worried about our parents because we are the center of their lives. I don't know what they're going to do when I leave for college."

Make sure that your children are not the center of your life. It's too much pressure on them, and it's not healthy for any of you. Simply remember these simple pillars: Love them, pray for them, teach them, and let them go.

* * *

Healthy mentorship looks like living like and glorifying Jesus in every area of your life. It starts at home; take care of your body's health, as it is a temple of God. Next to God, make your marriage your priority, and make space for your spouse, choosing them daily. Then tend to your children and family. You can't replace the time and attention that is necessary to flourish, but you can consciously surround yourself with good counsel that moves you in the right direction.

When your life is healthy at home, you'll have the energy and inspiration to step into the world to contribute to the marketplace and your community.

Water Walker Reflections:

On a scale of 1-10, rate yourself in each area of caring and respecting your body, then journal what you can do to improve:

FUEL YOUR BODY _____ How can I improve? _____
_____

MOVE YOUR BODY _____ How can I improve? _____
_____

STRENGTHEN YOUR BODY _____ How can I improve? _____
_____

LOVE YOUR BODY _____ How can I improve? _____
_____

My MIND HEALTH _____ How can I improve? _____
_____

My INNER HEALTH _____ How can I improve? _____
_____

MARRIAGE:
If you are not married, make your two "non-negotiable" lists:

WHAT YOU WANT: WHAT YOU DON'T WANT:

_____   _____

_____   _____

_____   _____

_____   _____

_____   _____

If you *are* married, journal some areas you can work on personally:

_____
_____
_____
_____

Share this chapter with your spouse. Journal some areas you can work together:

_____
_____
_____
_____
_____
_____

If you do not have children but plan to, journal your thoughts from this chapter:

_____
_____
_____
_____
_____
_____

If you have children, what are some areas you can work on your parenting: _____

_____
_____
_____
_____
_____

Ripple Effect:

Journal some ways taking care of your body, mind, and spirit will impact and be an inspiration to others: _____

_____
_____
_____
_____

Journal some ways having a Godly marriage will make an impact and be an inspiration to others: _____

_____

_____

_____

_____

_____

Journal the impact of how you are raising your children and how this will impact others: _____

_____

_____

_____

_____

Chapter 10

INFLUENCE IN THE MARKETPLACE

HAVING A CAREER is not just about putting food on the table or trading hours for dollars; we are *not* rats, and life is *not* a race.

A tremendous amount of thought and diligence should be applied when deciding on a career path; one that is aligned with your values and purpose. During the planning stages for this book, we held a *brain dump* session between my publishers, editor, and me. We met for three days at an inspiring Sonoran oasis retreat in Scottsdale to establish an accurate, principled foundation for the message of *My Mentor Walks on Water*. At this retreat, we also developed my *story arc*. This is a publishing term for discovering the essence of your message and the plot of your story.

But a brain dump and story arc aren't just tools for writing a book; they're incredibly useful for your everyday life. And, more importantly, they are helpful in establishing your trajectory in terms of a career. I encourage you to take some time to do a "brain dump" as it relates to your goals, values, and the type of legacy you want to leave. As you figure out your end goal, you can work backward to plot out your steps, crafting your personal story arc. Finding the right pathway for your career is worth the time and effort—regardless of how old or how far into your current trajectory you are.

That did not happen for me at the beginning of my career; there was no self-discovery process or brain dumping or thinking about a story arc.

It's important to know that just like I did, you *can* make navigational course corrections along the way, like a captain sailing a ship. The road to success is often under construction, which can involve quite a few detours along the way. Knowing this ahead of time can help you manage your expectations while still being hopeful for a positive desired outcome. When you hit roadblocks, it's important to press on and keep writing your story.

My high school guidance counselor informed me that since my family was AFDC (Aid to Family with Dependent Children), I was not college material. He said that because I had great typing skills, I should become a secretary. (Here's your reminder to not let people label you with *should*.)

Well, I listened. I became a secretary. The good news is, when we feel we've made a mistake, we can pivot! I quickly learned that being a secretary was not my passion, and later on, I accepted it as a detour.

Disclaimer: There's nothing wrong with being a secretary. I have friends who absolutely love it! They found their calling and are incredibly fulfilled and happy. For me? It simply was not a fit. I was a square peg in a round hole. I really disliked people telling me what hours I had to work, or when I could take a break or a vacation or get a raise. It wasn't that I was lazy; I have a strong work ethic. It was more of a growing awareness that I have a distaste for structure, cubicles, and punch clocks.

The life of an independent entrepreneur suits me perfectly. After a period of time working three jobs at once, I was eventually able to commit full-time as an entrepreneur. It wasn't easy, but it was worth it!

Success didn't happen overnight, but by staying consistent and diligent, and with the help of my incredible team, I have built one of the largest, longest-lasting organizations in the global direct sales/network marketing profession.

One of the things I love about our profession is the built-in mentorship within our business model. It's a "people business," which energizes me. You become successful by helping clients and other entrepreneurs, which creates a natural ripple effect. Except for having to be 18 years old, your level of education, race, gender, religion, or background is not a criterion. It is simply "do the do" and "work hard until ____," which means, like most jobs, compensation often comes long after your initial work. My philosophy is to "under-promise and over-deliver" because, while it is a simple business, it's not easy. I believe it's unethical to paint a picture that promises "get rich quick."

"If it's easy, it's sleazy."
—Rita Davenport

I like to say, "I am completely unemployable." Not having a boss is cool and all, but *cool* doesn't pay the bills. For many people entering into self-employment, this mindset turns into an even more destructive mindset: "I don't have to work, so I'll put it off."

Not everyone is meant for the discipline of self-employment. We encounter procrastination and distractions every step of the way. However, if you can master ruling over your career, you can avoid a boss ruling over you.

In general, our educational system primarily sets people up to get an education and then get a job working for someone else. With the soaring cost of university, it's great to see more emphasis on alternatives such as vocational and trade schools, apprenticeships and entrepreneurship. As you can probably tell, I love being a self-employed entrepreneur. It invigorates me, and it's rewarding to add value to others. I teach people about amazing products and how to network, share with others, and grow their businesses.

I absolutely enjoy what I do, and I'm so grateful I was able to send a thank you note to my guidance counselor (the one who suggested I become a secretary) with a copy of a book I was featured in called "Think & Grow Rich for Women." Sharon Lechter, CEO of "Pay your Family First" and co-author of "Rich Dad, Poor Dad," partnered with the Napoleon Hill Foundation and asked me to write my story. It's featured in the first chapter, between the stories of Mother Teresa and Oprah.

That said, never be afraid to step out of the boat if you know your career is not the right fit. Julia Child worked in secret intelligence before launching her first cookbook at age 50, pursuing her true passion and love: cooking.

Jeff Foxworthy followed in his father's footsteps, working nine-to-five in computer maintenance. He and everyone around him knew he had a natural gift for comedy. It wasn't until he was coaxed into entering an amateur comedy contest that he found his niche career. Today, he is regarded as one of the highest-selling comedy-recording artists, actors, and authors.

Take their stories and mine as your reminder: it's OK to pivot, change courses, and explore career options at any point in your journey. Simply go back to the drawing board, brain dump, and craft a new story arc!

3-DIMENSIONAL SUCCESS

So, what is *your* calling? What do you love to do? What puts a smile on your face? What are your natural talents? What energizes you? Discovering your unique career path according to your calling unlocks an invigorating level of passion and purpose. And it unlocks *true* success.

I like to call true success 3-Dimensional Success, or 3-D Success:

1. Creating and maintaining balance in your life
2. Making a difference
3. Financial peace

Let's take a look at each of these dimensions in more detail:

CREATING AND MAINTAINING BALANCE IN YOUR LIFE: When you're in a profession and industry that is the right fit for you, contentment and balance flow harmoniously. Seek this peace, and don't settle. As I mentioned in the previous chapter, however, make sure that your work matches your priorities for family first.

MAKING A DIFFERENCE: Don't just make a living; make a difference. Your career will be satisfying and meaningful when you are engaged in adding value and helping others. It creates a sense of significance knowing you are living in contribution, similar to the deposits in the emotional bank accounts I shared earlier.

FINANCIAL PEACE: 1 Timothy 6:10 says, "For the love of money is a root of all sorts of evil, and some by longing for it have wandered away from the faith and pierced themselves with many griefs."

It is not money itself that is evil; it's the *love of money*. Having a healthy mindset about money, such as living within your means, practicing contentment, and expressing gratitude brings financial peace. Concentrate on *true* riches, as temporal things tend to compete with eternal riches and obscure the knowledge of our priceless inheritance in Christ.

In thinking about 3-D success, allow this important principle of financial peace to be the foundation of your career—even if you are not ideally where you want to be.

In Napoleon Hill's book "Think & Grow Rich," the concept is to think and grow rich, not grow rich and think. Similarly, it's not to grow rich and give, it's to give and grow rich. It's not to grow rich and have integrity, it's to have integrity and grow rich.

I'll often have people say to me, "Donna, when I'm successful like you are, I'm going to _____ (fill in the blank)." The ones I hear most are:

- give to charities
- do the ethical thing and refer a client back to the appropriate business partner
- put that extra gift in a client's order

However, it's important to do those things now, not *after* you are successful—whatever success means to you. Remember: Do the right thing, in the right way, for the right reason. As your success grows, your giving and tithing can increase as well. Waiting to do the right thing "after" you're successful is not living with integrity.

FIRST THINGS FIRST

"I'd like to be remembered as one who kept my priorities in the right order. We live in a changing world, but we need to be reminded that the important things have not changed, and the important things will not change if we keep our priorities in proper order."

—S. Truett Cathy, Founder of Chick-Fil-A

I love the example S. Truett Cathy teaches about having his priorities in order: God, marriage, family, and business. Cathy established Biblical principles at the foundation of his business, including being closed on Sundays to honor God. While traveling through airports, I always notice that the longest lines are at Chick-Fil-A. God has blessed his business as a result of his priorities and obedience, and he is an inspiration for others to follow.

I truly believe that there is a revival happening in the marketplace community. Businesses want to have a meaningful purpose. Yes, profits are essential to stay in business, but genuine purpose is the generator of sustainability that makes businesses thrive through all the ups and downs—just like Chick-Fil-A. For this to happen, the marketplace must embrace the concepts of stewardship and discipleship. There are no shortcuts. The market is extremely savvy and educated, and consumers recognize a genuine brand from a fake attempt to speed-dial integrity.

Whether you are a stay-at-home parent, entrepreneur, employee, business owner, or volunteer, we set an example for discipleship and stewardship in our labor. Often, people are confused about these two terms, so I'll briefly explain. Discipleship is teaching Biblical precepts while modeling and guiding others toward living righteously as followers of Jesus.

Stewardship, on the other hand, is a bit harder to define. It's easy to think of stewardship only in relation to our finances and how we're honoring God through giving. While that is definitely part of it, stewardship involves much more. When we understand that *everything* we have was given to us by God in the first place, our mission becomes clear; it requires *all* of what we have and all we are. Stewardship is not only about finances; it's about our talents and gifts being poured out in service to others. We came into the world with nothing, and we leave with nothing.

MENTORSHIP IN THE MARKETPLACE

Society seems to compartmentalize a distinction between secular and spiritual careers. However, we are not to wear *church clothes* on Sunday for our faith and *work clothes* Monday through Friday for our jobs.

We are called to *love God* and *love people* around the clock—in church, at the ball game, at the gym, at work, and at home. Of the 132 public appearances of Jesus, 122 (over 90%) were in the marketplace. Forty-five of the fifty-two parables were marketplace context.

In his book, "The Marketplace Christian," author Darren Shearer tells his story of growing up as the son of a pastor and music minister, thinking that ministry was something that happened *inside* the walls of a church building.

His defining moment came while he served in the Air Force. God spoke to him and said, "Right now, your full-time ministry is on this Air Force base." After the Air Force, he attended seminary, studying practical theology to prepare for entering the business world.

What? Who does that?!

I love how Darren breaks the mold and explains that our theology is simply our understanding of God, whether you go on to be a pastor or work in non-profit ministry (like the majority of his classmates) or you pursue a career in business, which he has done successfully.

"Be imitators of me, just as I also am of Christ." (1 Corinthians 11:1)

Whether you're at your very first job bussing tables or the CEO of a Fortune 500 company, do others see Christ in you? Your workplace is your ministry as a witness to your faith. This doesn't turn off when we punch a clock. The people in your profession are already being discipled by somebody, for better or worse. You have a right to represent yourself and your beliefs; don't allow anyone to tell you otherwise. Secular humanism that promotes a godless worldview currently dominates the marketplace, and it's time to stand up and be like Jesus.

Jesus set this example for us when He discipled the 12 men who went on to impact the world. Through the letters of the church, we learn that Barnabas had a major role in mentoring Paul, who then had a big impact on Timothy. When you choose to be intentional in the workplace and pour into the people around you, teaching them about Jesus and using your influence for good, there is a massive ripple effect.

What would you like your ripple effect to be? I've been blessed with the ability to travel the world because of my career. Several years ago, I treated my extended family to a Caribbean cruise. We were quite the crew! For some, this was their first time venturing outside the state of Wisconsin. The trip had a significant impact on many of my family members: It not only sparked the desire to travel the world, but also passed on the entrepreneurial bug because of the testimony of my success.

As an example, my two nieces, Brianne and Danielle, were able to quit their full-time jobs and start their own business called Freshwater Design. They have a unique storefront/workshop boutique in downtown Augusta, Georgia, that pairs with a thriving online business. My twins, Liv and Alex, are herbalists and started their e-commerce brand, Good Counsel Herbs. All four of them worked other jobs while launching their businesses; however, one by one, they all were able to walk away from their full-time positions to dive headfirst into their new businesses!

The five of us are in a private message group titled "Success Tips with Mom/Auntie," where we interact and share regularly. I mentor them by sharing leadership, inspiration, and innovative business strategies.

The way we give ourselves to serve with our time, abilities, and finances reflects the way God gave himself to us and for us. What a blessing it is to know that our mentorship reflects the character and nature of God. This is our "kingdom assignment." Just like our children are constantly watching and learning from us, everyone we encounter at our workplace is as well! Your kingdom assignment is God's heart fully manifested in every area of your life.

Colossians 3:23-24 says: "Whatever you do, do your work heartily, as for the Lord and not for people, knowing that *it is* from the Lord *that* you will receive the reward of the inheritance. *It is* the Lord Christ *whom* you serve."

This scripture doesn't end in "except when you are working at your job."

You may not even know the full ripple effect your impact makes. Someone may not even know that they are your mentor!

This happened to me a few years back. At a conference I was attending, the speaker asked the audience to write down the names of three people they consider their mentors. Later, this speaker sought me out. She wanted to meet me as my name kept showing up as a top answer.

This surprised me because I've always considered myself to be under construction, wanting to still grow, learn, and be mentored. It was humbling to realize that while I am on a path for my own personal growth, people are looking up to me to follow my example. Keep this in mind as you are on your own journey. The mentee will one day become the mentor. I now understand and am willing, knowing that God has entrusted me to be an example. Protect and honor this responsibility. To whom much is given, much is expected.

"Shepherd the flock of God among you, exercising oversight, not under compulsion but voluntarily, according to *the will of* God; and not with greed but with eagerness; nor yet as domineering over those assigned to your care, but by proving to be examples to the flock." (1 Peter 5:2-3)

CHILDREN: MY BIGGEST CHAMPIONS

What if someone had been standing in the high school office with my guidance counselor and me and told us the story of my future self? We would not have believed it. No way!

Don't be afraid to have a *big vision*, and don't let anyone else snuff out your light. Years ago, as a young mom with three small children, I sat in a board room for a company sales training. The leader asked each of us to share our goals, and she started with me. I proceeded to enthusiastically share all the goals and aspirations I had for my business, building to the top of the company. One by one, each person proceeded to say, "Well, my children come first, so I don't plan on having those big goals." Those words cut like a knife, implying that *my* children didn't come first in my life.

I'm so grateful I didn't listen to the naysayers, and I want to tell you to do the same. Give yourself permission to have a significant vision for a great impact on the world, and tune out the noise that tells you otherwise. Follow your Holy Spirit TUG: The Ultimate Guide.

My children often share with me that, while they are grateful that they had tremendous educational experiences, some of their best teachings came from watching Mom (yes, me, with only a high school education) build a successful business from our home.

They watched me manage my disappointments, struggle with my daily tasks, and interact with people. My kids witnessed me setting audacious goals and missing them; however, then they watched me pick myself up, go for it again, and achieve them. They saw me fail and make mistakes, but they also saw how I learned from them and pressed on. Of course, these are skills they needed to learn and implement as they ventured into their adult lives.

In life, many will be at your podium recognition ceremony, but the most important people will be the ones who were with you at the starting blocks *and* during the race. You'll pick up more fans as you reach the finish line; I can promise you that. Don't let that distract or disappoint you. Keep your blinders on, knowing God has His hand on your back, nudging you forward.

My five children have been there through the good, bad, and the ugly. They have had a role participating in my journey *and* my success. I'm so grateful for my family; they share my success with me because we did it together.

To succeed in business, but fail at home, would not be success at all.

One of my favorite things to hear is when people tell me how special and kind each of my children is. I'll never forget when my oldest son, Nathaniel, had his wedding ceremony with my daughter-in-law, Shyam.

Nathaniel is a permaculturist, respected for the development of the Draw Permaculture Gardens, where the ceremony was held. He also regularly teaches visiting school children, interns, and even college professors, who want to learn from him. Current agriculture grows in rows with pesticides, while permaculture grows in God-ordained systems without chemicals and interference.

When the guests were arriving to the wedding, one said to me, "I'm so glad to meet the mother that birthed this amazing man."

CORNERSTONES OF SIGNIFICANCE

In Scott Hogle's book "Divine Intelligence: Discovering God's Wisdom for your Work Life," he shares:

> "Achieving success in the earthly realm is important, so don't ever let anyone tell you differently or try to shame you for your success. It is essential to your calling as it creates influence, wealth, and other necessary resources for you to complete the purpose of God in your life. Success can create money, but it can also pave a path toward significance when it is stewarded for eternal purposes."

The next step in the journey is to move from the stepping stones of 3-D success to cornerstones of significance.

"Success is when I add value to myself, but significance is when I add value to others."

The Law of Significance

Now, moving from success to significance didn't happen for me overnight, and it won't for you, either. Like much of what we've been talking about, it is a *process* to patiently accept and pass on to others. Let's take a look at what I believe to be the four cornerstones of significance:

TRANSPARENCY AND TRUST: Living a life of significance doesn't mean you're perfect. This road doesn't come without obstacles and failures, but we can learn from each other's journeys to avoid making the same mistakes. A big mistake prominent people make is attempting to come across as someone who doesn't fail; someone who is perfect and polished at all times. This is a set-up for discouragement because no one can live up to that. In fact, it's actually the transparency of revealing lessons learned in your own life through failure that builds trust.

A great tool is FEEL / FELT / FOUND: "I know how you *feel*; I *felt* that way too, and here's what I *found* that helped." This creates a pattern of trust that encourages and inspires others that they are not alone. Someone else overcame an obstacle they're facing, so they can too!

INTEGRITY AND HONESTY: There are no moral shortcuts if you value long-lasting significance. Cutting those corners will only create short-term success or failure. Instead, make a concerted effort to be patient with the process, and always operate with integrity and honesty. Be a person of your word—let your "yes" be "yes" and your "no" be "no." Have a because-I-said-I-would mindset. Don't lie, and be upfront about the things you're dealing with. These character traits are found in those who *become* and *remain* successful. I call this concept "the difference between a *shooting star* and a *rising star*." A rising star stays the course, while a shooting star is here today and gone tomorrow, quickly fizzling out.

SERVE AND ADD VALUE: It's important to maintain a servant mindset, no matter how successful you become. Be the person or brand that makes people feel valued. People don't care how much you know until they know how much you care. What are you known for? How can you add value to the lives of the people around you?

Rita Davenport says, "Pretend the people you meet have an invisible sign on their forehead that reads: *MAKE ME FEEL IMPORTANT.*"

WE *NOT* ME: People thrive when they are part of a tribe. Leaders of significance put people over profits, emphasizing a team-oriented, "better together" culture. It is crucial to establish an expectation of personal and team development, which, in turn, grows confidence and competence. By ignoring this, you create a performance lid that can cause stagnation and negativity. Empowered personal development is a cornerstone of significance.

These four cornerstones provide a blueprint for long-lasting success you can utilize not only in your personal mission statement, but also in the principles you instill in your workplace.

Above all else, know that God has a plan to prosper you and your business. This plan is a partnership, and proof of this can be found in Jeremiah 29:11: "'For I know the plans that I have for you,' declares the LORD, 'plans for prosperity and not for disaster, to give you a future and a hope.'"

And while many have memorized that comforting promise, many miss the actionable verse that follows in Jeremiah 29:12-13, "Then you will call upon Me and come and pray to Me, and I will listen to you. And you will seek Me and find Me when you search for Me with all your heart."

Yes, it's true that God *does* have plans to prosper you, but it requires *action* on your part. Seek Him with all your heart, call on Him and pray, and he will listen to you. This is the most powerful partnership you can have in your workplace.

Your influence and success in the marketplace will grow as you personally develop, grow, and implement these foundational principles along the way. Take some time to pray, dream, and discover God's amazing plan for your life. Regardless of where you are today, there is hope. Your calling may not be what someone else says you *should* do, but what you *could* do when you partner with the One who knows.

Water Walker Reflection:

Create your own brain dump and story arc: Take some time to answer these questions, then ask a friend or loved one that speaks life over you to brainstorm with you:

1. What is your calling?
2. What do you love to do?
3. What puts a smile on your face?
4. What are your natural talents?
5. What energizes you?

Where have you allowed someone else to "should" on you? Where can you make a career navigational course correction? _____

_____

_____

_____

_____

Take time to pray and ask Holy Spirit to make it clear what you *could* do with Him:

_____

_____

_____

_____

_____

When you read the definitions of discipleship and stewardship, where can you (or where are you currently) serving others with the gifts you've been given? _____

_____

_____

_____

_____

Who are the mentors in your life when it comes to the marketplace, and how do they influence you? _____

_____

_____

_____

_____

What qualities do you desire as you seek out more mentors in your life? _____

_____

_____

_____

Ripple Effect:

What would you like your impact to be on those you mentor in the marketplace? _____

_____

_____

_____

How can you lead a life of significance in the marketplace? What will you be known for? _____

_____

_____

_____

_____

Chapter 11

COMMUNITY INFLUENCERS

> "The value of life is not in its dura-
> tion, but in its donation. You are not
> important because of how long you
> live; you are important because of
> how effective you live."
>
> —Myles Munroe

ONE OF THE biggest misconceptions in our society is that our good works and charity are connected to a church building or ministry, and not an individual mission. For example, donating to the Red Cross or other agencies is a common practice when people feel prompted to give, or during an offering at their local church. However, as we've touched on throughout this book, the decisions we make and the steps we take are connected to our identity, what God says about us, our vision for legacy, and the foundation of Scripture. These promptings for giving should not simply be dictated to what church we attend or organization we feel compelled to support, but rather out of obedience to the call of God on our lives.

A helpful adjustment is regularly asking this simple prayerful question: "Heavenly Father, what can I do? Use me; show me your will. I am here; I am yours. I am willing and obedient to be used for Your good and plans. I am willing to give of my time and resources however you see fit. Amen."

I hope to encourage you to actively make this prayer a part of your everyday life; not by an obligation but rather a deep connection and motivation to make a direct deposit from your spiritual account—from your heart. This type of giving and good works are just two pieces of a much larger pie, and that pie is how we steward our influence and resources.

You are an influencer in your community—in your sphere. Whether it's your neighborhood, city, state, province, country, or the world, you have an influence where you're called. Your influence can be a handful of people or millions. God cares about each and every person you come in contact with, so why wouldn't He use you to touch them? To take this a step further, your impact on others can be in person *or* virtual.

With the advantage of technology, we literally have global access at our fingertips. In person, we can meet one-on-one, host a small group gathering, or gather in an auditorium;

however, we have access to influence millions of people around the world through the internet. Wherever your sphere of influence lies, whether it's in your neighborhood or online, consider what your impact on others could be. It's a huge responsibility to carry influence.

Why, you may ask?

Despite status symbols like blue checks on social media, hundreds of thousands of followers, fan mail, or applause, there is only One we answer to. One day, we each will be standing before our Heavenly Father—*alone*. We will be responsible for giving an account of how we influenced people. I'm telling you now, you don't want to be a stumbling block by influencing others *away* from the only One who matters.

Romans 14:10-13 says, "But *as for* you, why do you judge your brother *or sister*? Or you as well, why do you regard your brother *or sister* with contempt? For we will all appear before the judgment seat of God. For it is written:

'As I LIVE, SAYS THE LORD, TO ME EVERY KNEE WILL BOW, AND EVERY TONGUE WILL [a]GIVE PRAISE TO GOD.'

So then each one of us will give an account of himself to God. Therefore let's not judge one another anymore, but rather determine this: not to put an obstacle or a stumbling block in a brother's *or sister's* way."

Artist and songwriter Toby Mac got it right when he said, "I don't want to gain the whole world and lose my soul." Despite the accolades and applause of man, he knows what is most important.

I was recently cleaning out a drawer and found my very first Bible from 1978 after my encounter with Jesus. It's weathered, tattered, and torn with broken binding. I could barely read the faded poem I scribbled on the inside cover:

I AM MY NEIGHBOR'S BIBLE
(Author Unknown)
She reads me when we meet
Today he reads me in my house, tomorrow on the street
She may not even know my name,
Yet she is reading me

After all these years, I'm still struck by the impact of this profound message. I marvel at how this prophecy has and is playing out in my own life. I think of the little girl who was shamed for pink fingernail polish, the one who overcame many obstacles and setbacks to become a courageous, global influencer by simply being a living example of God's love. She would be proud of herself.

I love that the first Bible version I found was called "The Living Bible." As we read and encounter the Lord in His Word, we go out and live it!

An easy way to start stepping out to be a living Bible is to stop and pray for someone who shares about something they're going through. Typically, when someone brings up their pain or trials in conversation, our response is, "I will be praying for you." However, I encourage you to make a new habit of instead saying: "May I pray with you?" and right there, whether it's over the phone or in person, begin to pray.

Another simple way to live like Jesus is to be kind to people that are rude or stand-offish. The words "don't bother me" or "leave me alone" don't have to be spoken to be felt—they often radiate from people's eyes and energy. I challenge you to meet that message with a smile, a kind word, and an act of love.

YOU ARE AN INFLUENCER

Harriet Tubman once said, "You have within you the strength, the patience, and the passion to reach for the stars to change the world."

I hope you understand by now that, yes, you are an influencer, and you must use your influence to push people toward God. Harriet Tubman is a brilliant example of this. She was an escaped enslaved woman who became a conductor for the Underground Railroad, leading enslaved people to freedom before the Civil War, all while carrying a bounty on her head. She was also a nurse, a Union spy, and a women's suffrage supporter. Harriet relied on her unshakable faith in her Lord and Savior Jesus Christ and the protection of Holy Spirit to step boldly into her calling.

"The steps of a man are established by the LORD, And He delights in his way. When he falls, he will not be hurled down, Because the LORD is the One who holds his hand." (Psalm 37:23-24)

Harriet was an icon who influenced a positive shift in our society. We often expect this from other people, but how about you? Too often people dismiss themselves as unworthy of such grand influence on a global scale, so they don't even start.

I encourage you to pray and seek God's counsel about how He wants you to use your influence. The enemy wants you to feel hopeless and defeated, spewing lies about it being better to be isolated, further dividing the people of God. Listen instead to the voice of God to guide you, the voice of truth. From the beginning, God lived in COMMUNITY! He calls us to have unity and connection with others, gathering together to encourage and edify one another. All too often, we keep to ourselves, only caring about our own livelihoods and needs. That is simply not the way of Jesus.

Hebrews 10:25 says, "not abandoning our own meeting together, as is the habit of some people, but encouraging *one another*; and all the more as you see the day drawing near."

But where do you start? Well, earlier, I shared that your story begins at home and expands into the marketplace. You can start there, but don't stop there. You must continue to expand your circle of influence.

LOVE YOUR NEIGHBOR (LITERALLY)

Your story begins at home, then creates a ripple effect in your neighborhood, then your community, and, eventually, the world. So, let's start in our neighborhoods.

I find it startling how so many people don't even know their neighbors. You were put in the place you are for a reason! Don't wait for someone else to throw a block party or pot-luck—be the change yourself. Thomas and I regularly gather our neighborhood together, and it is amazing how many people express their gratitude that someone finally did *something*.

We've also established a group message thread to encourage and help each other. The messages range from something as simple as, "Does anyone have a cup of sugar?" to "How bad was the storm damage at your place?" It's an easy way to stay connected and check in on one another.

Over the years, we have found our neighborhoods have had a unique connection to the Native American community. Our home of 15 years in Arizona sprawled over 10 acres, directly across one of the largest washes in Cave Creek. After finding many artifacts, pottery, and petroglyphs, we did some research at the local library and discovered our home sat on a former bustling Native community.

Our current home is on the Menominee Indian Reservation and sits beside a lake in Northern Wisconsin. We started coming here in 1996, when we bought a vacation log cabin. We loved it so much that we found land just a few lots down and recently built our current home. Over the years, we've made friends with many of the members of the local Native community and enjoy learning about their culture and heritage. Their understanding of plant medicine alone is fascinating!

In preparation for this book, I asked for an interview with our friend Pasquinell, also known as Pas. He and his family have become close friends of ours. We noticed (and appreciated) how he instilled a strong family and work ethic in his children, moving away from a victimized or entitled mindset toward the values and honor of their indigenous heritage. The betrayal of and greed for colonization against their people is horrendous, yet Pas and his family set the example to rise above it all.

During our time together, he shared their story of moving from the Black Road to the Red Road (from dark to light) and his love for Jesus. He also recounted a Native tale that holds a powerful lesson for all who have ears to hear it: A grandfather once told his grandson of the two wolves that live inside everyone. One was a wolf of love, and the other was a wolf of hate. The two wolves constantly fight each other. When the grandson asked, "Which one wins?" The grandfather answered, "The one you feed the most."

Pas and I agreed that the unity between the Indigenous Nation and true Jesus followers is growing into a sweeping revival of healing for our nation and that we need to continue to partner in faith to see this happen.

"I am poor and naked, but I am the chief of the nation. We do not want riches, but we do want to train our children right. Riches would do us no good. We could not take them with us to the other world. We do not want riches; we want peace and love."—Chief Red Cloud

SHARE YOUR PIE

As we endeavor to expand our influence, we must be aware of the Spirit's promptings and nudges. If we're constantly on the lookout for what God might be calling us to do, we'd be shocked at how often He leads us to step out.

My friend Susan in Oregon recently shared with me that she felt a nudge to connect with a next-door neighbor who seemed distant. So, she baked a pie and took it over. Unfortunately, the neighbor wouldn't let her in when she knocked and simply barked at her to leave. Shocked at the response, Susan kindly replied that she hoped everything was OK and that she would leave the pie at the door.

When Susan arrived home from her errands that day, she found the pie sitting on her own porch. She simply said a silent prayer, and immediately thought of the nice family down the street with lots of kids. She was sure they'd love the pie! When they returned the empty pan, they gleefully gushed about how wonderful and thoughtful Susan's gesture was and how much they appreciated and loved the pie.

While this is an example of the little things we can do (and how we can turn a negative into a positive), I believe the *little* things are the *big* things. Don't judge whether something is of little significance or a major impact; just follow God's nudges and promptings. After all, the little things you do when no one is watching say more about your character than what you do when the world is watching.

Furthermore, your witness isn't something you turn on and off based on your activities. One of my husband's favorite expressions he shares is, "Never hold back an act of love." This

applies to giving a smile or kind word to a stranger or expressing your gratitude to your co-workers or loved ones. In every
interaction we have with those around us, we have a choice to
point to Jesus or not.

Recently, I was traveling from Sweden back home to the
U.S. Thomas was staying a few extra days for a training he was
speaking at in Oslo, Norway, so I was on my own. The morning we woke for my travel back across the pond, our airline
messaged me that my flight was canceled. They had already
rebooked me on a flight, but it was two days later, which just
so happened to be my birthday! Determined to get me home
so I could be with my family, Thomas spent almost three hours
on the phone working on a new flight with a different airline.
However, wouldn't you know it, the next morning, the same
thing happened. Canceled flight.

So, at 3:30 a.m., Thomas sat on the phone with the airlines
for another four hours, during the middle of which he was told
that I wouldn't be able to leave Sweden for four more days. He
patiently stayed engaged, helping me, even though he had a
busy week of work and preparation for his training. He stayed
calm and kind to everyone he spoke to while reassuring me that
everything would work out.

Thankfully, and without any extra cost to us, I was rebooked
through Paris in business class on my birthday. When I arrived
at the airport to check in, I, of course, met the same guy who
was trying to check me in the last couple of days. I greeted him
with a smile and cheerfully said, "It's my birthday; I'm finally
getting on a plane!" I tried to stay positive when I saw the look
on his face as he stared at his computer, not wanting to make
eye contact with me.

"I'm so sorry. The airline canceled your Paris to Detroit leg."

I took a deep breath, smiled, then said, "Of course they did!"

After a couple of minutes of furious typing, the impossible happened. "Wow. This is a miracle, but a seat just opened up on the Amsterdam flight. I'll put you there, and you'll get home tonight!"

In every encounter we had in that situation, Thomas and I kept our cool and were kind to everyone we spoke to. Knowing the busy schedule he had, I'm thankful that Thomas made a big deposit in my emotional bank account while not keeping score. He simply acted from a place of love and service.

Lastly, I want to encourage you not to just listen for God's nudges and promptings, but ask Him to speak! Simply ask, "God, as I go about my day, please lay the people you want me to reach out to on my heart." He will answer you, and sometimes you'll be startled!

My friend Cheryl recently shared that while at a restaurant with friends, another patron who was dining approached them and said, "God spoke to me and asked me to pray for you." She was looking at Cheryl's friend Sharon, who was having some health challenges. There was nothing visibly wrong, so there was no way she could have known that information apart from God. Holy Spirit knows things we don't know, so listen for His promptings and don't be afraid to act on them.

When I pray about this consistently, God always answers with names for me to reach out to. I often receive five or six at a time, so I simply jot those names down and either pick up the phone or leave a message saying something like, "God laid you on my heart. How are you? What can I pray with you about?" Often, people will say that my message came at just the right time. That's how God works. So, sprinkle random acts of kindness wherever you go. The world needs more of this!

"The smallest act of kindness is worth more than the greatest intention."—Kahlil Gibran

DON'T WAIT!

As I mentioned in the previous chapter, I often have people come to me and say things like, "Donna, when I'm successful like you, I'm going to create an animal rescue." I advise them not to wait, but to start now.

If God has laid something on *your* heart, then act on it! Don't let fear trap you or stop you from taking the first steps. You can start small, then build upon the foundation as your resources grow. Now, resources don't always equate to money. It could be connecting with the right people or tools, or the time to pour into the project.

And sometimes, those are the places of global impact.

Early in my career, I started Spirit Wings Kids, a 501(c)(3) charity supporting orphanages in India and Africa. It's incredible (and almost impossible to comprehend) that $700 a month supplies all the operational expenses for an entire orphanage. We do this through a partnership with Wick and Jan Nease, founders of Streams of Mercy Ministries. I trust and rely on them often, as they have a vetting process for matching resources with legitimate needs. As my business, resources, and income grew, I was able to increase my support.

On my first visit to our orphanage in India, I was using a piece of luggage that my twin daughters had used on a recent trip back home to Wisconsin at Christmas. When I arrived in Mumbai, I noticed two opened Christmas cards tucked in a side pocket, one for each of the girls. Inside each card was $70; a $20 bill they received from an aunt and uncle, and a $50 bill they received from their grandparents. My first thought was, *Wow, how did they miss this money? When I was a kid, we scrounged the drawers to find quarters for the ice cream truck!*

Then I had an idea. I called the girls and said, "Guess what I found in my luggage? Your Christmas money! I have an idea. Since you weren't able to travel with me to India, but your money did, I am going to document how far $140 of your Christmas money goes here."

They were in full agreement. Over the next few days, we had a videographer document just how far that $140 went.

In America, they could have bought a pair of jeans. Instead, they:

- Provided medicine for one full week in a slum community
- Patched a hole in a hut for a single mom where cobras were entering while her baby was slung from the ceiling
- Provided a meal for a group of kids living on the street
- Clothed an entire orphanage
- Sponsored a child to attend school

The impact this made on my family was priceless and profound.

If you put your hand out in front of you, you'll see that you have five fingers pointing out to serve other people. When you feel stressed or financially impaired, it's common to close down and pull in. If you close your hand into a fist, all five fingers are pointing back at you, and you are now cut off from the flow of giving and receiving. The blessings we receive aren't ours, they're ours to share. If we share our blessings with others, they multiply. In Luke 6:38, it says, "Give, and it will be given to you. They will pour into your lap a good measure—pressed down, shaken together, *and* running over. For by your standard of measure it will be measured to you in return."

Think creatively about the ways you can give and serve using your talents. At our orphanage in Uganda, a church donated some land and earmarked a section for us to develop a permaculture garden. This concept was new to Uganda, but my son Nathaniel was excited because he understood that because of the rich soil and abundant rainfall, Uganda would benefit from the permaculture principles of swales and growing in harmonious systems. He designed the garden, then taught them why it works and how to maintain it—long after he left Uganda. Today, it's a flourishing enterprise that feeds not only the orphanage, but the surrounding community.

Thomas was a professional soccer player and, with his contacts, was able to partner with the Swedish soccer community. They provided clothing and gear, along with our monetary support, to start a soccer academy at the orphanage. With Thomas's leadership and coaching, our orphanage team entered into a big soccer tournament. Giving these kids an opportunity to be part of a team helps keep them from getting into trouble and away from street drugs because they feel a sense of community and purpose.

Teenagers these days have found a way to skip forward and use social media to become instant icons. Suddenly, they are now considered world influencers; not because of the content of their character, but because of the number of followers they have.

You can't bypass the content of your character with blue checks.

Recently, a friend shared with me that he and his wife were at a prestigious resort. While there, they were told that the entire resort was taken over by the world's most famous social media influencers. Humored by this disclosure, my friend simply said, "OK, who are they? Let's check them out!"

As they strolled through the resort, they were surrounded by teenagers and 20-somethings, all barely dressed and constantly taking selfies. The whole ordeal was one giant party—hedonism into the wee hours.

Sadly, it's become the chief aim of many young people's lives to become the wrong type of influencer.

During the November 11, 2022, "60 Minutes" episode, they interviewed Tristan Harris, co-founder of the Center for Humane Technology. He shared that TikTok's Chinese creator limits what they put out in China. For instance, for viewers under 14 years of age, they show museum exhibits, science experiments you can do at home, Chinese patriotism, and educational videos. They also limit the consumption of TikTok to 40 minutes per day.

Harris stated: "They don't ship that version of TikTok to the rest of the world. China understands the influence technology has on people, so they provide the 'spinach version' of TikTok to China, while exporting the 'opium version' to the rest of the world, which has kids hooked for hours at a time."

Furthermore, there was a recent survey conducted by the Center for Human Technology that produced shocking results. When they asked Chinese pre-teenagers what they wanted to be when they grew up, the number one answer was "an astronaut."

Then, when they surveyed American pre-teens asking the same question, the number one answer was—you can probably see where this is going already—"an influencer."

Now, don't let this depress you; see it as the law of the vacuum. There is currently a void of true, honorable influencers and mentors, so it's our job to fill that vacuum. It is our job to fill it with true character and content that we can be proud of and carries on our legacy.

> "Your competence may get you in the room, but your character will keep you in the room."
>
> —Tommy "Urban D" Kyllonen,
> Rapper & Pastor of Crossover Church,
> Tampa, FL

THE MARKETPLACE IS MINISTRY

One day in 1983, the doorbell to my home rang. Upon opening the door, I was greeted by an enthusiastic teenager with an infectious smile and a teddy bear demeanor. This big, young guy looming on our porch was the one and only Bob Lenz.

At the time, I was a young mother of two babies, with one on the way. Bob and his brother, Bill, were just starting Solid Rock Ministries, the Jesus movement that swept across Wisconsin (and eventually the globe, with Life Promotions Youth Ministry). Bob was selling pizzas to fund their new ministry, and I was a busy young mom with big dreams to build my home-based business.

That encounter changed both of our lives. Of course, I bought pizzas, but more importantly, we forged a friendship that would span decades. Over the years, we would tease each other that he built a ministry, and I built a business to help support it.

Bob's ministry has gone on to impact millions of youths globally, in addition to starting Lifest, one of the largest global Christian music festivals. When we first met, I started donating as much as I could to the ministry. As my income and business grew, my support grew.

We had a profound moment together one day when we were backstage with the Newsboys. Bob honored and thanked Thomas and me as their biggest private donors. While they have had many large corporate gifts, we had been a steady contributor over the years.

However, the game-changing moment that weekend was when Bob asked me to speak. It was then that we both realized that Bob and I *each* have ministries. While his path was full-time physical ministry, my path was also full-time ministry in the form of success and influence in the marketplace. My role was not just funding his ministry but having a ministry to serve as well. God has given me a voice to witness and spread the gospel of Jesus in my own circle of influence. Since then, we have merged our ministries. It is no longer us and them; the ministry and the workplace. We all have a calling to share and demonstrate our faith.

So, what is *your* community impact? Where is your sphere of influence? Regardless of if it's a small group or millions of people, whether it's in-person or virtual, God is calling you to make a difference. Don't dismiss yourself! Take courage and step out of the boat.

Water Walker Reflections:

Too often people dismiss themselves as unworthy of such grand influence on a global scale, so they don't even start. What negative voices or beliefs are you holding onto or listening to that keep you from stepping out of the boat to be a true influencer? _____
_____
_____
_____

Rewrite your story: What step can you take today to influence those around you? _____
_____
_____
_____

Who can you influence in your family? Neighborhood? Community? Your place of business? At the gym? In your Bible study? At your kid's school? Globally? _____
_____
_____
_____

Ripple Effect:

Take a piece of paper and trace your open hand, fingers included. Then, ask God to put on your heart creative ways you can serve others using your gifts and talents. Write those ideas in each one of your fingers on your traced hand. Finally, ask a prayer partner to pray with you and hold you accountable in giving feet to these acts of service.

Chapter 12

CALLING WATER WALKERS

"If some among you fear taking a stand because you are afraid of reprisals from customers, peers, or even government, recognize that you are just feeding the crocodile, hoping he will eat you last."

—Ronald Reagan

TWO MONTHS BEFORE our family traveled to Uganda to serve at our orphanage and establish the permaculture gardens, a dear friend and leader in my business was tragically killed in Africa. Carol was with her family on a safari and was charged by a hippopotamus alongside a riverbank. Before leaving on our trip to Africa, I informed my family that under *no* circumstances would we go anywhere near a hippo!

I was reminded to be careful what I speak because we had countless hippo encounters during our trip. Our first was on a river safari; there were hippos everywhere, to the point of us even hitting them with our boat! After that, Thomas and I had an opportunity to take a gorilla trek in western Uganda. It was stunning to be above the clouds like in the movie "Gorillas in the Mist." Because our granddaughters were too young for the gorilla trek, we went alone, then stayed with them a few days later so our adult children Nathaniel and Alex could enjoy a chimpanzee trek. Little did they know, the entire trek was along a riverbank filled with hundreds of hippos. Alex was panicking while Nathaniel was calculating. Later I found out that the only words from their mouths were "Don't tell Mom" and "I think we can outrun everyone here."

Fear is real. We were probably right to fear the hippo encounters—it was a natural response! However, we often do all we can to avoid it.

It's no secret that the top fear people have is public speaking. That means most people would rather be in the casket than give the eulogy. *Yikes.*

Unfortunately, most people also have a fear of what other people think. That might even be at the core of why most are scared of public speaking. But what's interesting is that the foremost regret many have on their deathbed is that they wish they wouldn't have worried so much about what other people thought of them.

Other people's opinions of you are really none of your business.

That thought is easier said than done, and establishing boundaries that protect you from obsessing over other people's opinions can often take a lifetime to master. Don't wait for your deathbed to figure that out. Life is short, and discovering who you are is between you and your maker. Allowing other people to speak negatively into this part of your story is not okay. Furthermore, there's a difference between asking for feedback, input, and advice for support and someone casting judgment and authority as to what you *should* do. You do you.

As I often say, "Don't let anyone *should* on you."

Stepping out of the boat to walk on water and follow Jesus is going to require disagreeing with mainstream cultural norms. It's best to come to terms with this truth. It's healthy to realize we don't need to convince others we are right, nor be justified, in holding to what God has said. What God says matters most. Remember: One day, we will stand before *Him*. Not the people whose opinions we obsess over.

"Those who matter don't mind, and those who mind don't matter."

—Dr. Seuss

COME... COME

As you're moving forward in your journey, it will be helpful to remember that you are in this world but not of it. Keep your eyes on eternity and what truly matters. In other words, *think eternity.* You'll discover your circle of friends will evolve with you, and instead of discussing the latest gossip, episode on television, or movie star breakup, your circle of friends will love discussing prayer requests, sharing Scripture, swapping books, and talking about how God is moving in their lives.

Regardless of the country he's in or the size of his audience, my husband Thomas inevitably breaks the flow of his stage presentation to announce, "There's a book that I love to read, would it be ok if I share a story from this book? And the audience always goes "Yes." Then he proceeds to say: "In that book, there's a chapter called Matthew 14. It's about a long-haired guy, today let's call him J-C." Since Thomas himself is a long-haired guy, it's often followed by chuckles from the audience and a resounding "Yes!" He proceeds to share: "In the book of Matthew, Peter asks this long-haired guy J-C if he can join him and walk on water. J-C simply answers, 'Come... come.' Peter steps out of the boat to walk on water." Then, he goes on to share a whole training about that moment. One of his points is: "In life, you will have regrets [of both inaction and action]. One of the disciples walked on water, while the 11 others sat in the boat. Do you think Peter regrets stepping out of the boat to walk on water? Do you think the 11 others regret being boat sitters? What would *you* regret more, being a *water walker* or a *boat sitter?*"

I must admit that before meeting Thomas, I was *that* person who stayed in the boat. I was confident to speak of my faith when I was in church, a Bible study, or at a faith-based conference. Yet while I was in my other roles at work, community, and family, I operated in and lived out my faith in all

I did, but I didn't speak of Jesus confidently. I was the quiet Bible reader and silent prayer warrior.

Witnessing my husband be unafraid nor intimidated gave me the courage to use my voice. If this is your story as well, I encourage you to step out of the boat and use *your* voice. Do not be afraid. You will feel peace and congruency, knowing that you are not hiding your faith under a rock; you are letting your light shine, as in Matthew 5:14, "You are the light of the word—like a city on a hilltop that cannot be hidden."

I was pretty hard on myself when I realized it took me so long in my life's journey to discover this revelation. However, I then had to choose to be thankful that I did it—no matter how long it took! Everything awaits an appointed time and happens for a reason, all in God's timing.

> "For the vision is yet for the appointed time; It hurries toward the goal and it will not fail. Though it delays, wait for it; For it will certainly come, it will not delay *long*." (Habakkuk 2:3)

Give yourself grace; you are also on a journey, and every twist and turn along the way is a life lesson for you. What's most important is that you are growing. If you think of your maturing faith like your education, don't get stuck in kindergarten. You must eventually graduate to the next level of growth in your discipleship and maturity. For sports enthusiasts, think of it as moving from an amateur, to a professional, to a master, to eventually achieving legendary status, and leaving a legacy.

Of course, your journey will include stops and starts, setbacks and comebacks along the way. However, this is normal! Just keep moving. Keep putting one foot in front of the other.

We can all learn from Peter, who was the only one who stepped out of the boat to walk on water. Right there, in the middle of the waves, he took a step of faith toward Jesus. How often are we afraid to step out of the boat when we are in the middle of the waves in our own lives? Maybe it's something that feels impossible. Yet that is when we *must* take that step of faith. Peter didn't hesitate to step out; it was only after he looked down that he became afraid. He took his eyes off Jesus and began to sink! But Jesus was right there to lend a hand and catch him. No matter what your feelings are or what you're going through, take that step of faith and keep your eyes on Him. Jesus will meet you right where you are.

THE ALL-ACCESS PASS

I was recently drawn to a bold young woman named Jessi Green and found her podcast. My jaw almost hit the floor as she described a vision she had that was similar to my dream. (I'm amazed that this is how God works; He will give revelations, dreams, and prophecies to many different people to confirm His word.) While the vision in my dream looked similar to the parting of the Red Sea, Jessi described hers as seven waves of revival sweeping across our land.

She shares about how she was called to the beaches in California (among other places) to hold revival meetings, including worship and teaching and baptisms in the ocean. This movement is now called "Saturate." Jessi's call was similar to the call on my friends Daryl and Kristen to start their country church in their backyard.

In her book "Wildfires," she shares a story of traveling to Australia with her husband, Parker. Jessi stood on the edge of the ocean, praying, "God, Jesus, Holy Spirit, I want more of you, more of you."

Holy Spirit responded, "If I am the Pacific Ocean, would you want more of me?" And, of course, her response was, "No." Then He said, "It's like asking the Pacific Ocean for more ocean when you're completely covered and surrounded already by the waters. When you're in the middle of the water, you can't ask for more, because it's everywhere. It's all-consuming; you have it all. The choice really is, how deep do you want to go?"

How about you? Are you dipping your toes in the water when the entire ocean is available to you? At what point do you start to feel afraid and say, "This is as far as I go"? And, if you do venture out, each step you take as you wade in deeper is more uncomfortable, and the thoughts start to race: "Are there sharks? When I get to the point where I can't touch the bottom anymore, I'll feel out of control!"

Exactly. There *are* sharks in the water. (Metaphorical sharks, of course.) Your feet *won't* touch the ground, and you *will* feel out of control. You're abandoning yourself to whatever the Holy Spirit calls you to, and it will come with moments where you have to overcome fear and do it anyway. After seeing hundreds of people accept Jesus and be baptized, do you think Jessi regrets diving in?

Like Jessi, you have an all-access pass to Holy Spirit. He doesn't dole out portions; 10 percent to you, 40 percent to another, and so on. We are all given *full access* to a life in the presence of God. Think of it like the vast ocean I described above. Imagine that scene right in front of you. You have a choice: You can dip your toe in the water, or you can wade in deep and fully enjoy the rich blessings of His relationship with you. I challenge you to take that step of faith to tread in the deep, fulfilling waters God has called you to experience with Him.

Psalm 42:7 says, "Deep calls to deep in the roar of your waterfalls; all your waves and breakers have passed over me."

Deep calls to deep in the oceans of God's love. Surrender to Him as He calls you to a deeper faith. I believe that we must adjust our praying, "More of you, Lord, more of you." He's given us *all* of Him already. So instead, let's pray, "God, thank you for giving me all of You. Help me fully accept all You give so that I may give fully according to Your will. Let me be a vessel in which your living water flows freely back and forth between us, in Jesus' name."

"God provides the wind, but man must raise the sails."
—St. Augustine of Hippo

STEPPING OUT

The struggle to step out of the boat is real, yet there are millions of inspiring testimonies of overcomers to encourage us. From the eighth-grade student that stands up against bullies and teachers who tell her she has to apologize for who she is, to celebrities who come "out of the closet" to confess their faith in Jesus, there are courageous people all around us who are walking on water.

My friend Ray Higdon is a leader and trainer in my profession. Before he launched his successful RankMakers coaching business, he had worked his way out of foreclosure to become the top earner in his company. Despite his success, he knew something was missing. In searching for the answer, he spent two years doing meditations up to three hours long. Additionally, he sought out many kinds of therapy, doing the work to release the trauma of his past growing up in an abusive home.

However, he still felt the void—something was still missing.

He didn't know it at the time, but the hole he was trying to fill can only be filled by Christ! In November of 2022, he gave his life to Jesus. Since Ray has a huge following, he boldly stepped out of the boat and immediately did a live video on social media called "My Apology," where he shared his story and faith. What impressed me most was his sincere, authentic testimony. And God is using it in massive ways! Now, Ray goes live almost every day, professing his faith on social media and sharing lessons, Scripture, and his love for the Lord. He has received thousands and thousands of messages from people sharing about how he has inspired them. Of course, there were also some who didn't agree with his oh-so-public mentioning of God and Jesus. It took courage for him to take a stand for Jesus in front of hundreds of thousands of followers, and I am proud of him!

Another inspiring story comes from the rapper Eminem (Marshall Bruce Mathers III). He is considered one of the world's top artists even though, in God's eyes, he is just like you and me. God stands at the door of each of our hearts and knocks. Marshall felt God's knock for quite some time in his life. Troubled that his music masters forbade him from saying the name Jesus, he wrestled with his faith to write and perform the song "Walk on Water" in 2017 when he declared, "You can only walk on water when it freezes. I ain't no Jesus, I'm only human, you shouldn't believe in me."

Perhaps from the mentorship of fellow believer Kanye West, Eminem waded deeper into the waters to declare his faith in Jesus with his recent song "Declare This Gospel":

"So, my savior, I call on to rescue me from these depths of despair, So these demons better step like a stair, because He is my shepherd, I'm armed with Jesus; my weapon is prayer."

I love the last chorus of the song, as it's the punchline from being muzzled from his earlier song when he couldn't say the name Jesus:

"Blessings from the altar got me feeling like I'm walking on water."

Marshall took a bold step to stand up and speak out. There is a spiritual battle going on all around us, and the winner is usually the one who has the highest level of certainty in their belief, but only if they express it. The boat is crowded with sitters who are afraid to speak their truth for fear of the backlash and attack. So, stand up tall and boldly speak the truth in love. Know with all your heart and overwhelming certainty that you believe and know what you stand for.

Our world needs a movement of love- and truth-speakers to counter the boldness of the enemy's lies. I truly believe our society is dominated by like-minded, God-fearing truth-tellers who are muzzled and silenced. The sad part is, no one is holding them down. They choose to sit quietly on the floor of the boat as not to make any additional waves. In the meantime, evil lifts up a mighty roar, blowing waves of destruction because people are too afraid to engage.

It reminds me of Dorothy in "The Wizard of Oz," dropped off by a tornado in a strange land of witches and munchkins. Searching for a way to return home to Kansas, she's told she needs the help of the all-powerful Wizard. The final scene of the movie finds Dorothy and her entourage at the end of the Yellow Brick Road to meet the Wizard himself. The scene that awaits her is a bellowing voice behind a curtain on a grand stage with smoke and sound effects. The Wizard of Oz created a powerful illusion to frighten them away. Her dog Toto pulls back the curtain to reveal a small man with a microphone in his hand conducting the show, exposing the illusion. It turns out she had the way to get home with her all along: her ruby slippers.

It's the same for us. The enemy frightens us and creates an illusion, distracting us from the truth that what we need is already inside of us; the courage to look to God for help and invite Him in to save and guide us. The enemy is that Wizard behind the curtain. Don't be tricked by this tactic, as time is running out. We are never guaranteed even the very next minute of our lives.

As I write this chapter, earlier today, I attended a private virtual training event with Ed Mylett, and I am still reeling in disbelief as to what he shared. Last week, he had a famous comedian on his podcast. They were texting each other the next day about the success of the show, and a message came through at 10:20 a.m. on a Wednesday. The very next minute, Ed's guest died of a massive heart attack at 54 years old.

We often think we will have plenty of time to do that thing we've always wanted to do, or live the life we've always wanted to live, but we may not. The time is now. You have a choice to sit in the boat or step out of it to walk on water. What will you choose?

Together let's step out of the boat, putting a foot in the water that starts a ripple effect that creates momentum for a movement of Water Walkers. It starts with us.

Jesus says, "Come... Come."

Water Walker Reflections:

What are some excuses you've used to stay sitting in the boat? After each excuse, write an action statement to re-write your excuse and turn it into a step out of the boat to be a Water Walker:

EXCUSE: _____

_____

ACTION: _____

_____

EXCUSE: _____

_____

ACTION: _____

_____

EXCUSE: _____

_____

ACTION: _____

_____

Ripple Effect:

Journal how your taking action to step out of the boat and walk on water will impact others: _____

_____

_____

_____

_____

_____

_____

_____

_____

_____

EPILOGUE

INSPIRATIONAL WATER WALKERS

I PRAY THAT as you've read through these pages and worked through the content, it has stirred up a passion for Jesus and a deeper desire to both be mentored and mentor others. Before we part ways, for now, I'd like to share some of my favorite mentorship stories. I hope it inspires you to consider who mentors you, and how you mentor others. I'll end with a few exercises and journaling points for looking ahead at how you'll apply all you've learned as we've journeyed together.

LONDON, ENGLAND
Mentor: John Newton, 1725-1807
Mentee: William Wilberforce, 1759-1833

John Newton's mother, a devout Christian, died when he was 7 years old. At age 11, he started working with his father, a merchant ship captain and slave trader. Newton largely abandoned the faith of his childhood until the age of 23, when he nearly lost his life steering a ship through a fierce storm. John re-dedicated his life to Jesus and felt convicted of his profession, so he left it behind to become a minister in 1764.

While John Newton is famous for writing many hymns, including "Amazing Grace" (which described his life story), he was a mentor and influencer to William Wilberforce. Newton's remorse over his involvement in the slave trade inspired him to meet with Wilberforce, a member of the English Parliament who also grew up in Newton's church. Newton counseled Wilberforce to remain in politics to fight for anti-slavery rather than pursue becoming a minister. You could say Newton was mentoring Wilberforce to minister in the government mountain. Newton would remain a spiritual mentor for Wilberforce for the next 20 years before his death.

William Wilberforce would be considered a rebel in today's world. Similar to John Newton's story, even though William grew up in the church, he didn't have an encounter with Jesus until 1785 at the age of 26. Along with his encouragement from Newton, William's inner circle was like-minded and they became activists against the slave trade. However, he was mocked and criticized by the mainstream politicians and media of the day. I would guess that if he were alive today, he would be censored on social media for not being in lockstep with the progressive worldview. The majority did not want him stepping out to walk on water, but rather sit in the boat as to not make waves.

At a time many would have given up, he pursued his fight as the leading abolitionist for over 20 years to see the British Slave Trade Act of 1807 become a reality. However, he didn't stop there. It would be another 26 years before the complete abolition of slavery in the British Empire would be achieved.

William Wilberforce died three days after the passage of the Slavery Abolition Act of 1833.

Well done, good and faithful servants.

GERMANY
Mentor: Diedrich Bonhoeffer, 1906-1945
Mentees: Sophie Scholl, 1921-1943 & her brother Hans Scholl, 1918-1943

Opposition was scarce under the brutal Nazi regime of Adolf Hitler, as the atrocities and propaganda silenced the majority of Germans into fear and submission. However, there was one courageous young pastor, Diedrich Bonhoeffer, whose desire to speak up for a free society caused him to perform many acts of defiance. Just a few days after Hitler's rise to power, Bonhoeffer warned the German people about the dangers of the coming Nazi oppression during a famous radio address.

While most pastors submitted to the Nazi church, Bonhoeffer helped engineer the "Barmen Declaration," which stated that Christ was the head of the Protestant Church, not the Fuhrer. Realizing he stood alone against the Nazi influence, he moved to London for a two-year position at a German church which included a short visit to America in 1939. During his time abroad, he felt guilty that his influence was insubstantial. Bonhoeffer bravely returned to Germany, realizing it was the only way to affect change in his home country. He participated in several avenues of resistance, including joining military intelligence and plotting an assassination of Hitler in the early stages of the war. It was facilitating the escape of 14 Jews to Switzerland in the autumn of 1942 that led to his arrest by the Gestapo. Tragically, Bonhoeffer's execution took place on April 9, 1945, close to the war's conclusion. His last words were, "This is the end—for me, the beginning of life."

While Bonhoeffer recognized the dangers of Hitler during his rise to power, Hans & Sophie Scholl started the "White Rose Resistance" during the war's climax. They were raised in a loving Christian family. Their father was the mayor of their town and fiercely opposed Nazism. Like many rebellious youths, at the age of 12, Sophie joined the Nazi BDM (League of German Maidens), and her brother Hans joined the Hitler Youth, much to the disappointment of their father, Robert. Their father made a point to have long debates and discussions at the family dinner table. Their beliefs began to change slowly as they heard horror stories from friends serving on the eastern front, who witnessed Jews forced to dig their own graves, and in concentration camps. They also experienced the growing oppressive dictatorship in every area of their life, demanding loyalty to Hitler.

Sophie was forced to join the Reich Labour Force while Hans was sent to war. Hans and Sophie eventually made it to university, where they both met people who shared their views and discussed the ways they could resist the Nazi regime. Spreading the word to the German people through pamphlets and letters seemed to be the safest way to get the message across to the public. In total, the White Rose produced and distributed six pamphlets from 1941 to February 1943. The papers were derogatory about the Nazis, told stories of the atrocities of the war, and urged the public to resist. The "White Rose Revolutionaries," as they were called, including Sophie, Hans, and a group of friends would go to train stations, town centers, and universities at night to distribute pamphlets. When Bonhoeffer learned of the Scholl siblings, he would write and encourage them.

As they noticed more Germans waking up, they felt encouraged and emboldened in their approach. The morning of their arrest at the University of Munich, Sophie climbed the circular staircase for several stories at the entrance hall. At the very top, she dropped the pamphlets and watched as they cascaded like snow down the forum. They were immediately arrested, yet never gave up the names of the Resistance.

When asked to denounce their actions, they stood boldly. Sophie's final words were:

"I am, now as before, of the opinion that I did the best that I could do for my nation. I therefore do not regret my conduct and will bear the consequences that result from my conduct."

They were executed three days later by guillotine. Sophie's executioner said she never even flinched.

Sadly, that afternoon in Munich, they had a scheduled meeting with Diedrich Bonhoeffer that never took place.

U.S.
Mentor: Kathryn Kuhlman, 1907-1976
Mentee: Sid Roth, 1940-present

Kathryn Kuhlman's life and ministry is one of my greatest inspirations! Kuhlman was a faith healer and evangelist at a time when women rarely were allowed to preach. It's estimated that over two million people were miraculously healed through her ministry. She had a brief marriage with Burroughs Waltrip, who divorced his wife and left his two small sons after meeting Kathryn. Everyone in Kathryn's inner circle, including the internal tug of the Holy Spirit, told her *not* to marry him. She didn't listen and, sadly, regretted it from the moment she fainted during the ceremony. Waltrip kept her on the sidelines, silencing her voice as he took the stage, hijacking her ministry. Five years later, she had a defining moment that she refers to as her "death-to-self" experience. She went for a long walk and prayed and repented. Jesus comforted her as if it had never happened. She went on to preach but was often escorted from the stage before appearing, shunned for her "failed past."

Just imagine… this all happened in the 1940s! Kathryn would press on, knowing Jesus was the only perfect one and that she was forgiven. She would not be silenced. Many would sit in the boat, but she chose to step out and walk on water. Her finest years were after this difficult time in her life.

One of my favorite Kathryn Kuhlman stories is at her death. Her non-Christian nurses were tending to her when Kathryn informed them, "I shall die on February 20th at 1:13 am. Please have only roses at my funeral." Shortly afterward, the night nurse came to relieve the prior nurse, only to enter the room with the aroma of not a rose but what seemed like thousands. In fact, the scent of roses spread through the entire hospital. When noticing the monitor and time of death, it was exactly 1:13 am. Both nurses immediately began weeping, and at that moment, they gave their hearts to Jesus.

Sid Roth's "It's Supernatural!" talk show broadcast spreads across the U.S. and International Networks, and is now a popular podcast sharing how God is alive and well and supernatural! He also leads Messianic View Radio, established in 1977 and reaching millions of Jews through spreading the word of Jesus.

Sid was raised Jewish, but at the age of 32, after dabbling in New Age philosophies for several years, he became a born-again believer after a co-worker convinced him that Jesus is indeed the promised Messiah of the Jews. As a new believer, he met and developed a friendship with Kathryn Kuhlman. She interviewed him twice on her national television show and offered to mentor him as a new believer. One of Sid's regrets is not fully embracing her offer of mentorship, yet she stands as one of his biggest inspirations to keep following God's plan for his life.

Sid Roth is considered a mentor to hundreds of thousands of Christians globally. He is leading and encouraging the church of today to be a part of a sweeping great harvest revival during these end times.

Each of his mentees also mentor thousands more, creating a ripple effect of influence—just like Jesus, who started with 12 disciples, 11 of whom were instructed to share the great commission:

"And Jesus came up and spoke to them, saying, 'All authority in heaven and on earth has been given to Me. Go, therefore, and make disciples of all the nations, baptizing them in the name of the Father and the Son and the Holy Spirit, teaching them to follow all that I commanded you; and behold, I am with you always, to the end of the age.'" (Matthew 28:18-20)

U.S.
Mentor: Chuck Smith, 1927-2013
Mentee: Greg Laurie, 1952-Present

When Chuck Smith's mother was pregnant with him, his older sister was dying of spinal meningitis. Chuck's mother rushed her to her pastor to pray as she was taking her final breaths. She prayed that if God saved her daughter, she would devote her life to Him. His sister miraculously lived, and Chuck was born. It would not be until her deathbed that Chuck Smith's mother told him that she had dedicated him to the Lord.

She had him memorizing Bible verses as early as 4 years old! He was saved at 14 and chose Pre-Med studies to become a doctor. During college, however, he had a radical encounter with Jesus and prayed to God for clarity if he was on the right path. Chuck shares the story that God spoke to him and said, "Well, you can be a doctor and help heal people, but they will still die. Or, you can become a pastor and help people to receive eternal life."

While pastoring a church near the beach in Costa Mesa, California, during the late '60s, one of the greatest spiritual awakenings began to unfold. Chuck Smith encountered a community of teenage hippies led by Greg Laurie, and the "Jesus Movement" began. This movement went down in history books, impacting people for decades after (and still to this day).

The friendship and mentorship relationship between Chuck Smith and Greg Laurie, now one of the country's leading evangelists and authors, would also continue until Smith's death in 2013. Smith founded Calvary Chapel and planted over 1,000 churches nationwide, and the ripple effect carries on. Greg Laurie mentors many as Sr. Pastor of Harvest Christian Fellowship with campuses in Riverside, Orange County, and Maui. The Movie "The Jesus Revolution" is based on their story.

YOUR PERSONAL
MENTOR / MENTEE STORY

NOW THAT WE'VE looked at a few mentor/mentee relationships, as a closing exercise, I'd like to take some time to reflect on your own mentor/mentee relationships through a series of questions.

In this first section, you'll begin to write down some of your experiences in relation to mentors, including where you've been, where you are, and where you want to go. I encourage you to take out a journal* and make space and time to really think through these questions, even if you've answered some of them in another chapter. You might be surprised to see some of the answers change!

YOUR MENTORS

WHERE YOU'VE BEEN:

Reflect on the ways you've been influenced or mentored in the past. It could be as random as a book you read, a podcast or influencer you listened to, or a boss or friend. What are some of your "wrong way, Jonah" experiences, and what did you learn from them?

_____

_____

_____

Now, what are some positive mentorship moments you've experienced in your life? What did you learn from them?

_____

_____

_____

WHERE YOU ARE NOW:

Based on the Balance Wheel LQ (Life Quotient Test) in Chapter Eight, write the order of priority for growth. I.e., if you scored the lowest in Career, and the highest in Leisure, you would put a 1 by Career, and a 9 by Leisure, and so on.

Career _____   Leisure _____

Love Life _____   Friendships _____

Parenting _____   Community Contribution _____

Wellness _____   Finances _____

Spiritual _____

Don't be overwhelmed by the thought of how much work it might take to reach a balanced life. Take little steps, and don't forget to enjoy your progress! Find an accountability buddy (perhaps someone who has also read this book) and meet up for a meal or coffee (or virtually if they are not local) to compare notes, brainstorm ideas, and encourage each other. Make sure you leave that meeting with a plan by choosing two or three action steps to start moving.

Example: If your top need for balance was spiritual, you might have two action items:

1. Find a solid, Bible-believing local church.
2. Join a Bible Study (virtual or in-person) to make friends and be discipled in the Word.

If your second lowest score was career, then make a plan with your accountability buddy to explore career options that would be meaningful to you. Don't forget to set up a recurring meeting—accountability is not something that can happen sporadically. Try to plan for once a week or every other week.

Journal your plan of action: _____

_____

_____

_____

WHERE YOU WANT TO GO:

Remember, Jesus was the first Water Walker. You must keep your eyes on Him! The people around us, including mentors, coaches, and influencers, are human and make mistakes. Knowing this, what are some qualities and boundaries that you require to allow someone to influence or mentor you?

Examples:
- Follows Jesus
- Does what they say they will do
- Has proven success in the area you are looking for mentorship
- Authentic and honest
- Will hold you accountable
- Listens well

Journal your priorities for the areas in your life where you desire more mentorship, and make a list of your non-negotiables. Then, find a mentor (if you haven't already), set a goal, and execute a plan of action to achieve your desired outcome.

_____

_____

_____

_____

MENTEE

As you've seen in my story, often you will discover that while you are being mentored, you are naturally mentoring others. Your journey creates a natural ripple effect and impacts the people around you. However, we must be intentional in how we mentor. In this section, we'll again look at where you've been, where you are now, and where you want to go as it relates to mentoring others.

WHERE YOU'VE BEEN:

Can you think of any areas from your past where you may have influenced someone or others down a wrong path? Again, it may have been because you were on the wrong path or direction personally. Whatever the story, journal your experiences (and forgive yourself if necessary).

_____

_____

_____

_____

On the flip side, journal about a few positive mentoring moments you've been on the giving side of: _____

_____

_____

_____

_____

WHERE YOU ARE NOW:

Who are you currently mentoring, or whom do you have influence over? Take some time to think about whether or not you are leading from the right place currently. If not, what are some steps you can take now to course correct? Journal your thoughts and make a plan of action to execute that plan.

_____

_____

_____

_____

_____

WHERE YOU WANT TO GO:

Congratulations! Today is the first day of the rest of your life. Do not give the pen of your story to someone else, as your future story is yet to be written. As we wrap up, take some time to journal the story of your future self. What would be written about you? What impact would you like to make on others? What imprint will you leave long after you are gone? What is your legacy? The journey is yours to take. With the guidance of our Heavenly Father through Scripture, the Holy Spirit, and the ultimate Water Walker, Jesus, and the help from others that you choose wisely for mentorship, the path before you is full of potential. May your favorite words to hear be:

"Well done, good and faithful servant."
(Matthew 25:21 ESV)

CLOSING

Jesus is the ultimate teacher, but so much more than a mentor. He is the savior of the world that much of the world has rejected. Will you? He stands at the door to each of our hearts and knocks. Those who invite Him in as Lord of their life are saved. "Think Eternity." Where will you spend eternity? You must answer this most important question. We are called to be fishers of people. Continue to spread the Good News and bring others with you. Share this book, start a conversation, and continue a Water Walker Movement.

*Water Walker Journal & other Merchandise available at www.mentordonnajohnson.com

All proceeds go to Spirit Wings Kids 501C3

NOTES

NOTES

NOTES